THE CHRISTIAN TORAH

KINGDOM LIVING ACCORDING TO THE KING'S STANDARDS

APOSTLE CYNTHIA V. WHITE

The Christian Torah Kingdom Living According to the King's Standards

Published by Fruit That Remain Publishing LLC
1282 Smallwood Drive W #195
Waldorf, Maryland 20603-4732
Voice (301) 868-4314 - Fax (301) 868-7326
Web address: http://www.fruitthatremain.com
E-mail: cvwhite@fruitthatremain.com

ISBN 978-1-934326-02-2
ISBN 1-934326-02-X

Published in the United States of America

Brentwood Christian Press
4000 Beallwood Avenue
Columbus, Georgia 31904

DEDICATION

This book is dedicated to my children, Myrna, Walid, Gregory Jr., Lance, Nikki, Brandon, Kalika, Denise, Larry, and Laura. You all have been a part of my learning process of becoming a good parent, and you have taught me in the natural what I had to also learn in the spirit. You are a very important part of my life, and I appreciate your support and patience while I was attending school, working, and preparing for ministry work. You all are a great blessing to me, and you also provide a great deal of encouragement to me to continue my writing projects. I am appreciative of all of your efforts to assist me in this project and other areas of my life. I thank each one of you! I also appreciate God for giving me a wonderful group of children. Each one of you is a special gift from God, and I will always cherish all that you have shared with me all of these years.

CONTENTS

FOREWORD

The Christian Torah is a wonderful work that my spiritual daughter, Cynthia White, has received the revelation on. There are times when we as a people need something we can live by, something that will guide our lives. God sent it through Jesus Christ when He sat down and taught His disciples on the mount. People in every generation need principles by which they can live. The principles in this book will take you from one level of living to another of kingdom living. The principles that Jesus talked about were lessons on everyday life. I can see why Cynthia called this book "The Christian Torah." Under the old covenant, the people of that time put on things that were called Phylacteries, which they wore on their heads or on their hand as something to aid them in prayer and stay in constant remembrance of what God said.

In this book we learn the things that God says we need to do in order to have success in life. It is imperative that you read this book and come into the next level of living: kingdom living. As you read this book, you'll identify the thought pattern of Jesus, be able to tap into His mind, and think through His thoughts. All of this is possible when you understand the Beatitudes in which Jesus walked, lived, and breathed. Jesus understood that if He was going to change the heart of His disciples, who were killers, sinners, thieves, and highly educated people, He was going to have to instill in them something that would prevail against all they had in them prior to meeting Him. Jesus knew everybody could change, if given the right principles.

This book offers the right principles that are taken directly from the Word of God. I have just a little advice for you: read it, meditate on it, and live it. Remember these words from 2 Timothy 2:15: "Study to sh[o]w yourself approved unto God, a workman that needeth not be ashamed, rightly dividing the word of truth." James 1:22 says, "But be ye doers of the word, and not hearers only, deceiving your own selves." Once you have read the book, then meditate on the words you've read and process them. Let them get down deep in your heart, because it's there that you begin your change. May you embrace the promise given in Joshua 1:8: "This book of the law [torah] shall not depart out of thy mouth; but thou shalt meditate therein day and night, that thou mayest observe to do according to all that is written therein: for then thou shalt make thy way prosperous, and then thou shalt have good success."

Prophet Rodney S. Walker DD

APPRECIATION

I am very appreciative of all of my brothers and sisters in Christ who participated in the surveys that I conducted to gather data for this book. I would also like to take this opportunity to thank Gail Cherochak dba Paper Treasures, Fruit That Remain LLC, God Is In Control Church, Bishop Rodney S. Walker Sr., Union Bethel AME Church, Rev. Dr. Harry L. and Sherita Seawright, the Maple Springs Baptist Bible College and Seminar, and Brentwood Publishing for your support and assistance in the preparation of this book for publication. I appreciate your willingness to meet the challenges necessary to complete the final preparation for printing and distribution. Your ideas and suggestions contributed immensely to the success of this project. It is good to have you as part of the team. I am confident that good things will come from our joint efforts. Thank you again for a job well done.

CHAPTER 1

INTRODUCTION

Some Christians today are living defeated lives because they do not know or understand the instructions that Jesus left for them. Others know and understand the instructions but do not obey them because they do not realize that they are citizens of the kingdom of heaven and not of this world system in the earth, and this fact alone defeats them. Many are miserable because they are trying to be like the world, and they don't fit into the world. They are in the world, but not of the world. The world loves only its own; therefore, the only way to be loved by the world is to be like the world. Christians live in the kingdom of heaven, with Jesus Christ being the King and Lord of the kingdom.

Jesus has provided instructions for the kingdom and its citizens. It is not possible to enjoy the full benefits of the kingdom if you don't know that your king has rules and regulations pertaining to kingdom living, responsibilities, rewards, benefits, and justified consequences. It is also important that Christians understand all of the instructions of the kingdom because they complement each other. These instructions include rules and regulations for successful living with God, their immediate family, their Christian family, and the community. If these instructions are not known, then Christians cannot enjoy the fullness of all that God has provided for Christians' success here on earth.

The instructions that Jesus left for Christians are found in the Book of Matthew in the following five sermons:

- The Sermon on the Mount, given to a large crowd—Matthew 5:1–7:27
- Instructions to the twelve chosen by Christ—Matthew 9:35–10:42
- Parables of the kingdom given on a crowded beach—Matthew 13:1–52
- Instruction to the community given to the disciples—Matthew 18:1–35
- The Olivet Discourse given to the disciples—Matthew 24:1–25:46.

These five sermons are known as the "Christian Torah." *The Word In Life Study Bible* describes the teaching of Christ that presents the application of truth in day-to-day life as the "Christian Torah," the five major speeches that Jesus recorded in the Book of Matthew. The Christian Torah is to Christians as the Pentateuch (the five books of the Old Testament, known as the five books of Moses, also called Torah) is to the Israelites. The Christians' Torah served the same purpose as the Israelites' Torah: to teach God's people to hear and do what God commanded.

The Christian Torah contains detailed instructions for the followers of Jesus Christ concerning the nature and the character of the world in which they live, the attitudes to exhibit, and the do's and don'ts in relationships with one another, with the general public at large, with the community, in business practices, and in financial pursuits. Jesus talks to His followers concerning their spiritual status in this world and in His world (the kingdom of heaven). Jesus mentions in His prayer to His Father concerning Christians (John 17:14) that He had given them the Father's Word, and the world hated them because they were not of the world even as He was not of the world. Jesus also mentions to His followers in John 15:19 that they are not of the world. In verse 19 He tells them, "If ye were of the world, the world would love his own: but because ye are not of the world, but I have chosen you out of the world, therefore the world hateth you." Jesus expresses this point again in John 17:6–9 when He mentions to the Father the separation of those who belonged to God. Jesus' teaching in the Christian Torah is a sharp contrast to the teaching of the world and also a sharp contrast from the customary life of God's people.

The instructions given in the Christian Torah are specific to life in the kingdom of heaven. The kingdom is expressed and realized in the spirit and the heart of the followers of Jesus Christ. Jesus said to Pilate in John 18:36, "My kingdom is not of this world: if my kingdom were of this world, then would my servants fight, that I should not be delivered to the Jews: but now is my kingdom not from hence." And Pilate answered in verse 37, "Art thou a king then?" Jesus answered, "Thou sayest that I am a king. To this end was I born, and for this cause came I into the world, that I should bear witness unto the truth. Every one that is of the truth heareth my voice." These truths that Jesus talks about are expressed in the Christian Torah. A person must be a part of the kingdom of heaven in order to know and understand the truth. Jesus mentioned this to Nicodemus, a ruler of the Jews and Pharisees, saying, "Verily, verily, I say unto thee, Except a man be born again, he cannot see the kingdom of God" (John 3:3). Nicodemus thought that Jesus was talking about the natural birth of this world, but Jesus explained further in verses 5–6, "Verily, verily, I say unto thee, Except a man be born of water and of the Spirit, he cannot enter into the kingdom of God. That which is born of the flesh is flesh; and that which is born of the Spirit is spirit." This told Christians that they are to live in a spiritual kingdom and not just in the natural physical place.

Kingdom living requires that people repent and turn from what they are currently doing (Old Testament or pagan worship) to what Jesus (as King) is asking them to do now (New Testament worship).

Are We Following the Christian Torah?

The teaching of Jesus in the Christian Torah gives the acts, the deeds, the behavior, and the consequences of living in Jesus' kingdom, where all Christians reside. Therefore, Christians—of all people—should know and live by the kingdom's principles. Do Christians know these principles? Are they living according to the Christian Torah?

Matthew 4 records the beginning of Jesus' public ministry, which started immediately after His encounter with the Devil. During this encounter with Satan, one of the first ordeals that He encountered was hunger. When the Devil tried to tempt Him with bread, Jesus said something amazing in Matthew 4:4: "It is written, Man shall not live by bread alone, but by every word that proceedeth out of the mouth of God." Since Jesus is God, it is certain that He intended for man to live by His words. The next thing that Jesus said prior to calling His first disciples was recorded in Matthew 4:17: "Repent: for the kingdom of heaven is at hand." These two statements were made before He preached the first of the five sermons that make up the Christian Torah. Therefore, special consideration should be given to these statements. Christians must understand what Jesus commanded them to do and also understand that they can't fully operate in the kingdom (the world that they live in) if they do not understand its rules, requirements, and benefits. Jesus wants His followers to follow Him; however, this cannot be done outside of the kingdom where He reigns as King.

Why Obeying the Christian Torah is Important

Some Christians do obey the Lord, and some are living according to His plan for their lives. Many obey the Word of God to the best of their ability, but they are limited by what Christian education teaches them. Most of the Christian teaching does not include the Christian Torah. I believe that people in the church know more about what the apostles (especially apostle Paul) said than what Jesus said. Many of the New Testament writers repeat some of what Jesus taught in the Christian Torah; however, none of them taught the commands and principles to the extent and detail that Jesus taught them in the five sermons of the Christian Torah.

The Christian Torah is a fundamental, foundational part of our instructions for living and functioning here on earth. It is absolutely necessary for Christians to realize and understand that God has prepared an environment for living that will ensure the fullness of the abundant life that Jesus talks about in John 10:10, which says, "The thief cometh not, but for to steal, and to kill, and to destroy: I am come that they might have life, and that they might have it more abundantly." The word "abundantly" in this passage of scripture means "exceedingly great, very high, or beyond measure." If the thief is going to come, then Christians must be prepared to live in a place where the thief cannot penetrate. Since Jesus Christ Himself has defeated the thief, Christians must know that Jesus wants His followers to live in a place that is a safe haven for them here on earth. This scripture tells us that Christians will have to deal with trials, tests, afflictions, or persecution; however, they do not have to be defeated by these challenges. They do not have to hang their heads and live in a state of being broke, busted, and disgusted all of the time. Christians cannot stop the Enemy from coming. As clearly seen in Psalm 91:1–9, evil tidings will come, but the LORD protects His people from the fowler and the pestilence. The LORD encourages His own not to be afraid of the terror by night or the arrows of the Enemy by day, for He says that a thousand shall fall at their side and ten thousand at their right hand, but no harm shall come to His people, but they shall see with their eyes the reward of the wicked. All of this is true because God's people have made Him their habitation. Similarly, Jesus Christ has prepared a place of habitation for His followers that is safe and secure from the wiles of the Devil, and that place is the kingdom of heaven over which He is King and Lord. Christians who do not understand and practice His teachings of the Christian Torah are not able to live in the fullness of the abundant life that Jesus has prepared. The purpose and the concept of the Christian Torah is to define a place of habitation for born-again believers.

Questions Addressed in This Book

This book answers the following questions:

1. What is the Christian Torah, where is it located in the Holy Bible, and what is its connection with Christians?
2. What did Jesus instruct regarding how Christians should live, as found in the Christian Torah (Jesus' five sermons found in Matthew)?
3. What are the benefits of the Christian Torah?
4. Did the first century church comply with Jesus' instructions as found in the gospel of Matthew?
5. Do current-day Christians understand the instructions given by Jesus as found in the gospel of Matthew?
6. Do Christians daily live in compliance with the instructions given by Jesus?

7. What are some of the reasons Christians give for not following Jesus' instructions?

What This Study Covers

This study was limited to the teaching of Jesus in the gospel of Matthew. However, it may be supported by these same sermons of Jesus as recorded in the gospels of Mark and Luke. In addition, the study was supported by a questionnaire of a small sample of current-day Christians to answer the study questions and validate the study findings. The study was also limited to the opinions and the findings of the author from the sources listed in the bibliography.

As you read this book, you may find it helpful to consult the glossary in the back of the book for explanations of biblical terms.

CHAPTER 2

WHAT CHRISTIAN LITERATURE SAYS ABOUT THE CHRISTIAN TORAH

Being born again into the Christian family (the body of Christ) is a new beginning for all who make that choice. It's a new place, a new attitude, a new spiritual position, and a new lifestyle. All of these new situations require training and instructions about how to live and grow in the new environment. Jesus gave all of the necessary instructions during His time here on earth. One of the wonderful things that He left for us is the Christian Torah—instructions for Christian living and information about its benefits. Christian living is a very beautiful endeavor. Belonging to God and living according to His will are the most wonderful things that can happen to a person. This chapter examines the literature and provides information regarding the instructions and benefits that are found in the Christian Torah.

John the Baptist, the prophet of God, had preached many times to tell people to repent because the kingdom of heaven was at hand. John prepared the people to receive Jesus Christ and what He had to say to them. After John was sent to prison, Jesus knew that it was time to begin to teach the people what they should repent from and what they should turn to. And from that time on Jesus told them, as recorded in Matthew 4:17, "Repent: for the kingdom of heaven is at hand." The Word came forth first in the message of the sermon.

Sermon on the Mount (Matt. 5:1–7:27; Luke 6:20–49; Mark 4:21–23; Luke 8:16–18; Mark 10:2–12)

The Sermon on the Mount is the longest of the five sermons studied in this book. Because it is a long sermon, the reader tends to get off the subject of what Jesus was teaching His followers. This sermon taught the character of the followers of Jesus, gave examples that represent the required character, and encouraged Jesus' followers to pursue this character. The character that Jesus presented to His followers was the central issue of the sermon, and it was presented to them within the culture and social environment that was present during that particular time in history.

The character changes that Jesus presented in this sermon were radical changes compared to the lifestyle of the religious leaders at the time. The people needed an example to follow, or perhaps a role model, to give them a clear picture of what God expected of His people. Prior to the birth of Jesus, the people were looking to the scribes and the Pharisees to teach them the way of the Lord. However, Jesus said that the righteousness of His followers must exceed that of the scribes and the Pharisees.

Jesus wanted His followers to understand that obeying His words by pursuing the character traits that He taught required a heart change, not an outward obedience to a set of regulations and traditions. This outward expression of righteousness is what the scribes and the Pharisees were doing, and it did not represent what Jesus had in mind. Richard Coleman, Sloan Lyman, Andrew Sloan, and Cathy Tardit, the authors of *Sermon On The Mount: Examining Your Life,* give a very good example of this in their book. They wrote about a sect of Pharisees that was known as the "bruised and bleeding Pharisees." These men were so religious and so concerned about holiness that they went to great extremes in order to protect them-selves from sin. They would blindfold themselves in order to protect themselves from any thought of lust that they might encounter if they by chance looked at a woman. This action resulted in their bumping into things and get-ting cuts and bruises that led to their nickname, "bruised and bleeding Pharisees." It was good that they wanted to live a holy life, but Jesus was asking them to take the more radical approach of getting their hearts involved. Jesus knew that the heart is the key; living a life accept-able to Him involved a heart change. He mentioned this in Luke 6:45, "A good man out of the good treasure of his heart bringeth forth that which is good; and an evil man out of the evil treasure of his heart bringeth forth that which is evil: for of the abundance of the heart his mouth speaketh." The "bruised and bleeding Pharisees" were not trying to be victorious of lust; they were trying to do something on the outside to keep lust away and let the inside stay desolate and void.

Edwin K. Broadhead, the author of *The Sermon on the Mount and Grace*, confirms the purpose of this sermon. He presents the Sermon on the Mount as a pattern of the lifestyle that belongs to those who follow Jesus. The Book of Matthew makes it clear that the call to discipleship (you must be saved) precedes the demands of the sermon. Following His baptism (Matt. 3:13–17) and His temptation (Matt. 4:1–16), Jesus began a ministry of preaching in which His message was this: "Repent, for the kingdom of heaven is at hand." (Matt. 4:17). At that point Jesus called His first disciples (Matt. 4:18–22). With these disciples He went throughout Galilee preaching the gospel of the king-dom, teaching, and healing (Matt. 4:23). As a result, crowds from many places followed Jesus (Matt. 4:24–25).

Thus, Matthew chapters 5–7 present the teachings as instruction in discipleship. The description and demands of the Kingdom are given to those who have already come under the claim of the kingdom. Consequently, the Beatitudes and the material that follows should not be understood as requirements to be met, accomplished, or achieved in order to find God's acceptance; they represent instead the demands God places upon those who have entered into the way of the kingdom. As noted in Broadhead's book, New Testament scholar Edward Schweizer concludes, "That the Sermon on the Mount from Matthew, as well as the Sermon on the Plain from Luke, begins with the Blessings reveals the awareness that only God's gracious encouragement…can stand at the beginning."[1]

The first section of this sermon contains the Beatitudes. The word "beatitudes" is translated from a Greek word that means "blessed." Blessedness is a state of spiritual well-being and prosperity. This is not a state of utopia with no choices, nor is it an unrealistic state for future generations only. It describes a place of being for the present and the future. The Beatitudes describe a covenant relationship (with God) that has practical application rather than an emotional state of being or attitude. The blessedness of the Beatitudes is explained by action and the result of action taken.

Bill Dodds and Michael J. Dodds, authors of *Happily Ever After Begins Here and Now—Living the Beatitudes Today*, agree with this definition of the Beatitudes. They write:

By definition, a beatitude is supreme happiness. The word beatitude comes from the Latin word, beatitudo, which means happiness. The point

19

here is that when we read the word blessed, we need to understand that it means happy, as in complete, made whole, satisfied, and at peace rather than a skewed notion of holy, as in grim, stern or solemn reverence.

But aren't those who are truly holy—in the best and most accurate sense of the word truly happy? Of course. That's what the Beatitudes are all about. That's what Jesus was explaining to his listeners "If you are this way ... or "If this happens to you because you are this way ..." then you will be given the kingdom of heaven, the earth, Satisfaction, Mercy and all those other good things.

The beatitude (happiness) we are promised confronts us with decisive moral choices. It invites us to purify our hearts of bad instincts and to seek the love of God above all else. It teaches us that true happiness is not found in riches or well-being, in human fame or power, or in any human achievement—however beneficial it may be—such as science, technology, and art. Or indeed in any creature, but in God alone is the source of every good and of all love.[2]

In addition, Stuart Briscoe, the author of *The Sermon On The Mount—Daring to Be Different*, writes that Jesus, in the Sermon On The Mount, expressed principles and moral, ethical, and social behaviors that came from His eternal mind and that have to do with men and women of all ages. This is a part of what makes Christians distinct and different from the world. Jesus gives these instructions to His followers as the attitudes to be adopted. In other words, as Christians we are to have the following attitudes:

- **Be poor in spirit (live in humble dependence on God).** Being poor in spirit will cause you to be blessed with the kingdom of heaven. If you depend on God and give your will (acknowledge the need of spiritual transformation from the poor state that exists without God being in control) to God, you will have the kingdom of heaven with all the rights and privileges therein. Dodds and Dodds, authors of *Happily Ever After Begins Here and Now: Living the Beatitudes Today,*[3] write that the poor in spirit were those who admitted they were helpless without God, the ones humble enough to accept the fact that they weren't in charge.

- **Mourn (feel the pain of your sin, the sin of others, and the sin of the world).** If you mourn, you will be comforted. Stewart Briscoe, the author of *The Sermon On The Mount—Daring to Be Different,* lets us know that this does not just refer to those who sit at a graveside, but much more, to those to whom repentance comes deep in the soul when we realize all God has in mind for us and how little of it we have appropriated. "There is no fulfillment for those who reject the truth about themselves. We must come to a brokenness, contrition, and confession before God."[4] When we are willing to admit that we sometimes do sinful things and are broken and sorrowful about them, repenting with our hearts, God will comfort us, refresh us, and heal us in those areas. Otherwise we will continue to be led by our own lust that leads to the sin that brings consequences that eventually lead to death. As is written in James 1:15, "Then when lust hath conceived, it bringeth forth sin: and sin, when it is finished, bringeth forth death."

- **Be meek (be known as gentle, humble, and courteous).** This will cause you to inherit the earth. According to Sinclair B. Ferguson, "The word meek is the humble strength that belongs to the man who has learned to submit to difficulties (difficult experiences and difficult people) knowing that in everything God is working for his good. The meek man is the one who has stood before God's judgment and abdicated all his supposed 'rights.' He has learned, in gratitude for God's grace, to submit himself to the Lord and to be gentle with sinners."[5] God has proven in the recording of the history of His people that no one can stop Him from giving the earth to those whom He chooses. Egypt could not keep Israel, nor could the residents of Canaan keep the children of Israel from possessing the land.
- **Be merciful (treat people with kindness and mercy).** If you are merciful, then mercy is what you will get when you need it. If you give mercy to others, then God will be merciful to you even when others do not want you to have mercy or kindness. Michael H. Crosby, the author of *Spirituality of the Beatitudes—Matthew's challenge for First World Christians*, writes that mercy is a sign of God's perfection and care. Crosby describes mercy as "an outpouring to others of God's gift of mercy that we have experienced. When my spirituality expresses this fifth beatitude, I manifest compassion, con-

cern, and care for every human being. This quality of mercy enables me to become a brother or sister to everyone in the world in such a way that I share God's very blessedness."[6]

- **Have a pure heart (let your life be an open epistle with no deception or hidden motives, and be a person of honesty and integrity).** This type of action will cause you to see God. God will move in your favor. You will not have to ask. To see God means that He will make Himself seen to you.

- **Be a peacemaker (bring peace to personal and social situations by being actively involved in bringing resolution to conflicts and offenses whether you are at fault or not).** This will cause you to be seen as a son of God, a person who exhibits his or her character and operates in the fruit of the Spirit. A peaceful environment is very important for the operation and flowing of the Holy Spirit. According to James 3:18, "The fruit of righteousness is sown in peace of them that make peace," and Galatians 5:22 reminds us that peace is a part of the fruit of the Spirit: "But the fruit of the Spirit is love, joy, peace, longsuffering, gentleness, goodness, faith." Therefore, being a peacemaker is very important in kingdom living.

- **Be willing to be persecuted for righteousness sake (be joyful and exceedingly glad when men say all manner of evil against you falsely and when they revile you).** When you are willing to be persecuted for righteousness sake, great is your reward in heaven. You will have a rich reward with God. Jesus reminds us here that the prophets of God were treated badly because they obeyed God.

Therefore, we should expect the same kind of treatment. We must know, however, that God will reward us here on earth just as He did the prophets of old.

- **Be the salt of the earth (in the natural world, salt seasons, purifies, and preserves).** We must be like salt and season the world with God's ways and His purpose for the earth. In addition, we must be soldiers of the kingdom of God, fighting all who come against God. We must fight evil so that God can keep decay and death from things that belong to Him.
- **Be light (be the light that brings life and drives out the works of the darkness).** You are the light by which the world can see God. Your purpose as light is defeated if you try to hide the light; therefore, be out in the open so the light that you have can be seen.

After the discussion of the Beatitudes, Jesus talks about the relationship between Himself (Jesus Christ) and the law. Jesus explains that He is the one who will fulfill the Old Testament law, and He goes on to say that His Kingdom is manifested through character and mission. Jesus was not trying to do away with the law; He was saying that He was the person sent by the Father to fulfill all the requirements of the law. Therefore, the requirements of the law would no longer be able to separate those who believed that Jesus is God, resurrected Savior, and Lord from God.

Once Jesus' followers understood that they were saved from the penalty of the law, they could obey the commands of the kingdom and participate in the promises of the kingdom. Jesus stressed that His followers must be more righteous than the scribes and the Pharisees, whose standards were based on an outward expression of religion rather than an inward expression of the heart.

After Jesus relieved their minds of having to meet the requirements of the law, He began to talk to them about practical life issues. Jesus connects the issues of life with the heart. This is clearly seen in Proverbs 4:23, which says, "Keep thy heart with all diligence; for out of it are the issues of life." In others words, Jesus says the kingdom is a spiritual place where the intent of the heart is paramount. The old covenant, Jesus reminds them, required a change of outward action only, but this new covenant (kingdom living) is based on a change of inner actions (a heart change).

Before He gives them the kingdom principles, Jesus tells them what the law required and follows that with what the Kingdom requires. Richard Peace, Layman Coleman, Andrew Sloan, and Cathy Tardif, the authors of *Sermon On The Mount: Examining Your Life,* report that this comparison is called "antitheses." They write the following concerning the comparisons mentioned in Matthew 5:20–48:

> "Jesus' startling statement in verse 20 sets the stage for this and the following five sections (5:27–30, 31–32, 38–42 and 43–48), in which he illustrates the nature of the righteousness that surpasses that of the scribes and Pharisees. These sections are known as the six antitheses, so called because each begins with the formula "You have heard…. Followed by "But I tell you….." In each case, Jesus focuses his audience to consider the real meaning of the law. While verses 17–20 emphasized his discontinuity with its interpretation. Actually, the term "antithesis" is a bit

misleading since Jesus is not contradicting all of these statements. He does not say that while the law prohibited murder, now it is all right to kill anyone who bothers you, nor does he say that while adultery used to be wrong, now it is all right to indulge one's sexual fantasies without limit. Lapid suggests that they should be considered "Super theses" rather than "antitheses" since Jesus is intensifying the meaning of the law. In this particular section, Jesus addresses the meaning of the commandment not to murder. While the scribes had reduced the meaning of this command to simply a prohibition of the actual act, Jesus reveals that its intent is to expose the murderous desires that are found in instances of anger, insult, ridicule and conflict. To accent its meaning he offers three examples of murderous relationships (5:22) followed by two illustrations meant to encourage the active pursuit of reconciliation.[7]

Therefore, Jesus is admonishing His followers to pay attention to the character traits of the kingdom because they are the responses expected of each believer. He continues to talk about anger with a brother, adultery, divorce, oaths, vengeance, and love. Of these He said the following:

Anger—Since this word in the Greek (orgizo (or-gid'-zo) means to provoke or enrage, such as to become exasperated, it suggests a deep-seated inner anger rather than a hot temper flash. Jesus tells His followers that they must not be angry with their brother without cause, because, as Jesus taught, anger was considered to be like killing under the old covenant, when the consequence of killing was judgment. Now, Jesus says, you will be in danger of judgment if you merely say to your brother in anger without cause, "You fool," or make a statement that indicates the worthlessness of your brother and accuses him of being apostate from God, according to the authors of *Sermon On The Mount: Examining Your Life.*[8] Jesus says that this person will be in danger of hell fire, which when allowed to continue would cause a person to be consumed by the very anger that the person intended for another. Jesus wanted His followers to focus on reconciliation with each other (their brother) rather than retribution. Thus, since we all as Christians have only one Father God, we must understand that Father's love is the same for all. Therefore, Jesus is saying that you must love your brother, He is not going to take sides with you against your brother, and the kingdom does not work that way. In fact, Jesus tells us that if we want to bring an offering to God, we must go to our brother and reconcile with him. Leave your gift, He says, and come back once you have accomplished the reconciliation. Finally, Jesus tells us before leaving this point to agree with our adversary quickly while they are still willing to talk about the issue. Do not wait until you have to go to court and have to deal with the judgment. You are only in danger of judgment as long as there is a chance for reconciliation. Jesus says if you wait for judgment you will surely go to jail. This, of course, gives the followers of Jesus a clear picture of their having to stand before God with an unacceptable explanation if they refuse to reconcile with their brother. God is Father of both; therefore, it is not possible for one child to go to the Father with complaints and attitudes about a brother or sister and not deal with his or her own attitudes. Also, God is Lord of both; therefore, we are not going to be able to invoke favoritism on our behalf.

27

Adultery—Jesus tells His followers that this is no longer an outward act. If you look at a woman in lust, you commit adultery. This is best expressed with the situation of the bruised and bleeding Pharisees who believed that they could avoid lust and adultery by not looking at an inviting woman. Jesus wanted all who followed Him to realize that there must not be a desire in their hearts because that is the kingdom's standard.

Divorce—Jesus begins this "super-theses" by reminding His followers of the laws of Moses regarding divorce. The original intent of the laws was to protect the wives from abuse from their husbands. This was needed because men were allowed to have more than one wife and even concubines, but women were allowed only one husband, lest they commit the act of adultery. Jesus knew that the men were used to having the opportunity of having more than one wife; therefore, He taught them God's heart concerning marriage and divorce. The original law was in place to protect the woman because a man could never be guilty of adultery, but a woman could unless properly divorced by her husband. Jesus is now telling His followers that the man is now responsible for his ex-wife's adultery should she remarry because he divorced her.

Oaths—Jesus taught His followers the importance of keeping their word by letting their "yes" mean yes and their "no" mean no. Jesus was letting them know that they did not need to swear by anything to keep their word. Jesus wanted them to know that oath taking was not an indication of honesty or integrity. Therefore a person is not required to make oaths. Jesus is saying to them, "Just tell the truth. Let your 'yes' mean yes and your 'no' mean no. Anything else comes from the Devil."

Vengeance—(Old Testament, Lev. 24:20; New Testament, Matt. 5:39) Jesus reminds His followers that the Old Testament covenant dealt with the judicial punishment of an eye for an eye. But now Jesus wants enemies to be loved and forgiven by man because the Lord says that vengeance is His. Paul mentions this in Romans 12:19: "Dearly beloved, avenge not yourselves, but rather give place unto wrath: for it is written, Vengeance is mine; I will repay, saith the Lord." Therefore, we should leave the vengeance to God.

Love—Love is a key ingredient in this New Testament covenant that Jesus was presenting. The kind of love mentioned in this passage is agape. In this sermon Jesus gives two directions concerning love. The first is an explanation of God's heart concerning their enemies. The Old Testament (Deut. 7:1–2) gave direction to God's chosen people concerning their enemies. Moses told them, "When the LORD thy God shall bring thee into the land whither thou goest to possess it, and hath cast out many nations before thee, the Hittites, and the Girgashites, and the Amorites, and the Canaanites, and the Perizzites, and the Hivites, and the Jebusites, seven nations greater and mightier than thou; And when the LORD thy God shall deliver them before thee; thou shalt smite them, and utterly destroy them; thou shalt make no covenant with them, nor shew mercy unto them."

The Israelites followed directions to the best of their ability, but they did not know the heart of God. God wanted them to love Him and hate evil. He wanted them to be an example of His love in the earth. Now, Jesus says in Matthew 5:44, "But I say unto you, Love your enemies, bless them that curse you, do good to them that hate you, and pray for them which despitefully use you, and persecute you."

This command must have been a hard direction to follow. After many years of being able to give retribution to offenders, Jesus' followers found that the door was suddenly shut. I can imagine that they must have said what we say sometimes when God chastises us: "Is this really God?"

The second direction that Jesus gave His followers concerning love is, "Love thy neighbor." This is one of the most powerful acts that a subject of the kingdom of heaven can perform. The apostle Paul gives an explanation of this in 1 Corinthians 13:13, "And now abideth faith, hope, charity, these three; but the greatest of these is charity." According to the Bible there is no greater command from God than to love Him and our neighbors. These commands are found in Matthew 22:37, Mark, and Luke 10:27. Jesus said in Mark 12:30–31, "And thou shalt love the Lord thy God with all thy heart, and with all thy soul, and with all thy mind, and with all thy strength: this is the first commandment. And the second is like, namely this, Thou shalt love thy neighbour as thyself. This none other commandment greater than these." Jesus is implying here that keeping these two commandments will empower you to keep the other commands mentioned in the five sermons discussed in this book.

I can imagine the thoughts that might have been going through the minds of people who were used to retaliation being approved even for persons classified as their neighbors. Therefore, in Matthew 5:39, Jesus makes it clear by instructing his followers not to resist an evil person. Jesus goes on to state some remaining conditions that require actions of love.

He tells them not to resist an evil person. These evil persons may or may not be their neighbors; nevertheless, Jesus tells them not to fight back. Many believe this type of attitude and behavior would indicate timidity. However, Jesus wanted the actions of His followers to always be directed by love. He gives examples, such as letting people strike them more than once without retaliation in any manner. He admonishes the people not to even retaliate in court. Jesus knew that many of them were expecting a king to take control of the land from the Romans. The Romans had a law in place that forced the local citizens to carry their belongings for up to one mile. Jesus makes it clear that love was the standard measurement for all decisions and actions. Therefore, with that Roman rule in mind, he tells them not to fight the civil authorities, commanding in Matthew 5:41, "And whosoever shall compel thee to go a mile, go with him twain." The next words that Jesus says to them are even more astounding. In Matthew 5:44, he tells them to love their enemies. Jesus knew that they were used to the rule of loving their neighbors and hating their enemies; therefore, He says in Matthew 5:43–44, " Ye have heard that it hath been said, Thou shalt love thy neighbour, and hate thine enemy. But I say unto you, Love your enemies, bless them that curse you, do good to them that hate you, and pray for them which despitefully use you, and persecute you." Jesus goes on to let them know that it is now time to repent (turn from their old ways) by praying for their enemies and doing good to them that hated them, for this is a characteristic of His followers and also a way to be identified as children of God. Jesus is letting them know that love should be the motive for everything that they do.

From this point Jesus goes on to talk to them about being boastful about their giving, fairness, and honesty. People learn by example, and the religious leaders at that time were being very visible about their giving, praying, and fasting. They wanted people to know what sacrifices they made so as to receive public commendations. Therefore, the people of God believed that this was the way that they should be. In addition, people in authority were taking advantage of the poor, overlooking the widows, and collecting more taxes than the Romans required and keeping the extra for themselves. In the midst of these abuses, Jesus let them know His heart on the matter. In Matthew 6, Jesus let the people know that He desired that the giving be done from the heart because of love. Also, praying should not be just a public show; they should also pray in secret and not let people know that they were fasting. Jesus commanded His followers to repent and turn from the old ways and follow His example.

In the middle of this sermon Jesus taught them how to pray. His prayer format was very clear in terms of the change that His life was bringing to the people of God. He taught them to pray to the Father, to hallow (to set apart, to consecrate, or to make sacred) His name, to pray for His Kingdom to come and His will to be done on earth as it is in heaven, to request daily bread, to forgive those who sin against them, to lead them not into temptation, and to deliver them from evil, acknowledging that the Kingdom, the power, and the glory belong to God.

From this point Jesus talks about the kingdom law regarding riches. He warns them to lay up treasures in heaven and not in the earth, for the treasures of the earth will rust and are subject to thieves breaking in and stealing them, but the riches in heaven are eternal. Again Jesus reminds His followers that the walk with Him is all about the heart. He mentions riches in Matthew 6:21: "For where your treasure is, there will your heart be also." He goes on to tell them to watch what they look at because the eyes give light to the body; therefore, they are to keep their eyes focused on the light so that the body will be full of light. Jesus declares that if the light of the eyes is darkness, how great that darkness is.

At this point Jesus has given His followers information that seemed to be hard to do compared to what they used to have to do. Therefore, He comforts them by telling them of His Fathers' good pleasure to give them all that they need to live if they focus on the kingdom of God, because the Father knows all that they need, and all of it will be added to those who seek the kingdom first. It is interesting that Jesus reminds them of how the Father takes care of the birds even though they do not sow or reap. This indicates that we should be sowing and reaping because Jesus speaks of their importance in this passage. Not only will the sowers get what they need, but they will also get a harvest from what they sow. Jesus goes on to tell them to take no thought of what they shall eat or drink, or of the clothes that they need, because their Father in heaven knows what they need. He tells them to seek first the kingdom of God.

If all of this were not enough Jesus continues by giving a lesson about judging others. Jesus lets them know that they can no longer have a condemning attitude concerning the problems and faults of others because that same attitude will be used to judge them. Jesus teaches them to never give pearls to swine. This is one that Christians forget quite often because they expect unsaved people to act like saved people. They get angry when they come in contact with people who do not exhibit the fruit of the Spirit, not realizing that the people cannot even understand what the Bible is saying if they are not saved. Therefore, they treat the pearls of the kingdom of God like swine; if it's not good for food, they disregard it and often belittle the giver and pronounce the giver's Christian walk as useless. Like Father, like son; if the Holy God is the Father of Christians, then they should be like Him. If Satan is the father of the unsaved, then they should be like him. We cannot expect anything else.

As Jesus gets ready to close this sermon, He encourages His followers to pray continuously by asking, seeking, and knocking, telling them that what they need will be given, that what they seek is available to them, and that the door will be opened to them. Jesus encourages them by letting them know that God is not like man (man is basically evil) and God is good; therefore, if they, being evil, know how to give good gifts to their children, how much more a good and loving God will give to His children. Now, Jesus tells them to do unto others as they would have done unto themselves. This command has to do with sowing and reaping. Many Christians do not make the connection; therefore, they do not understand that what they do is sowing, and anything that they plant is going to come up after its own kind. Therefore, Jesus told them that whatever they want done unto themselves they should do to others because they will get back what they give.

Jesus now gives them an understanding that all of the commands that have come forth in this sermon lead them through a narrow gate and down a narrow path that leads to true life. He warns them not to choose the wide gate and wide path that lead to hell. There is no more opportunity to worship God without considering the condition of the heart. No longer would outward sacrifices be sufficient.

Jesus warns them of false prophets and tells them (via the metaphor that good trees produce good fruit, and evil trees produce evil fruit) that anyone who does not produce good fruit will be cut down and burned; therefore, they should be careful of those who are teaching something other than what He has told them.

Instructions to the Twelve (Matt. 9:35–10:42, Mark 6:5–13, Luke 9:1–6)

Before Jesus began to preach this sermon, He called His twelve disciples and prepared them to be sent forth by giving them power to cast out unclean spirits and to heal all manner of sickness and disease. He gave them instructions for service. The following is the list given to them:

- Go only to the lost sheep of Israel. Since Jesus had come to be Savior and Lord of the nation of Israel, they were told to evangelize their own first. Jesus was indeed the Messiah that was promised to Israel by the Prophets of the Old Testament. Jesus gave the nation of Israel the first opportunity to receive the good news of the kingdom of heaven. They could receive it or reject it, but they could not say that they were not given the opportunity.
- Preach saying, "The kingdom of heaven is at hand."
- Take no gold, silver, or brass in your purses or clothes because the workman is worthy of his meat.
- In whatever city you go to, if they are open to receive you, stay until you deem it necessary to leave. When you enter a house that is open to receive you, let your peace come upon it, but if that house is not open to receive you, let your peace return to you. If that city or house does not receive you or hear your words, shake the dust off your feet and move on. Michael H. Crosby explains the importance of this instruction to the apostles. According to Crosby, "The gift of God's power and peace, which the disciples received in Matthew 10:1–7, was to be shared with every community, house, and person. 'Look for a worthy person in

every town or village you come to and stay with him until you leave. As you enter his home bless it. If the home is deserving, your blessing (eirene— peace) will descend on it, (Matthew 10:11–12).' The initial activity of the first evangelizers was to extend the blessing of peace. God's power is experienced in blessing. The blessing is *'eirene;'* peace. The disciples were told at the Mount of Transfiguration to listen to Jesus (Matthew 17:5) so the world that will not listen to the disciples' proclamation of God's way of peace and be evangelized (see Matthew 10:40–41) will lose the peace once given in Matthew 10:13. When a society rejects the justice and order that leads to peace, that society receives Jesus' reproach (see Matthew 11:20–24; 23:33–39)."[9]

These instructions so far seem to be all in favor of the cities, towns, villages, and people being evangelized. There was no room for self-indulgence, self-pity, or self-concern in these instructions. This was certainly a radical difference in what the Israelites were used to doing. To follow these commands meant a complete self-sacrifice. This was not all, because Jesus knew that no matter how great the sacrifice, there would also be persecution. This persecution would be at a level that none would expect from people receiving the good news of the kingdom. After all, the Israelites were all expecting a king to come from the line and the kingdom of David as was mentioned in Mark 11:10, "Blessed be the kingdom of our father David, that cometh in the name of the Lord: Hosanna in the highest."

Therefore, after giving these instructions to His apostles, it was necessary for Jesus to warn them about persecution and the possible negative receptions from some of their brothers and sisters who would be given the opportunity to hear the good news of the kingdom of heaven. Jesus warned:

- I send you forth as sheep among wolves; therefore, be as wise as serpents but as harmless as doves.
- Beware of men because they will deliver you up to the councils, and they will scourge you in their synagogues.
- You shall be brought before governors and kings for my sake for a testimony against them and the Gentiles, but take no thought of what you will say, for it shall be given you that same hour what to speak, for it is not you who speak but the Spirit of your Father which speaks in you.
- Brothers shall deliver up brothers to death, and the father, the child. The children shall rise up against their parents and cause them to be put to death.
- You shall be hated of all men for my sake; however, you who endure to the end shall be saved.
- When they persecute you in this city, flee to another. I will come before you have finished visiting all of the cities in Israel.
- As a disciple you are not above your master, nor as servants are you above your lord. If they have called me, the master of the house, Beelzebub (the name of Satan), how much more shall they call those of my household?
- Do not fear what is covered or hidden, for it shall be known.
- What I tell you in darkness, speak in light, and what you hear in the ear, preach upon the housetop.

- Do not fear those who kill the body but are not able to kill the soul, but rather fear him who is able to destroy both soul and body in hell.
- Two sparrows are sold for a farthing and shall not fall to the ground without your Father. Know that the hairs on your head are numbered; therefore, do not be afraid, because you are worth more than many sparrows.
- Whoever confesses me before men I will confess him also before my Father which is in heaven, but whoever shall deny me before men him I will also deny before my Father, which is in heaven.
- I have come with a sword; I did not come to send peace. I have come to set a man at variance against his father, daughter against her mother, and daughter-in-law against her mother-in-law. A man's foes shall be they in his own household.
- Those who love their father and mother more than me are not worthy of me. Likewise, he who loves son or daughter more than me is not worthy of me.
- He who will not take up his cross and follow me is not worthy of me.
- He who finds his life shall lose it, and he who loses his life shall find it.
- He who receives you receives me, and he who receives me receives he who sent me.
- He who receives a prophet shall receive a prophet's reward, and he who receives a righteous man shall receive a righteous man's reward.
- He who gives even a drink of water to one of these little ones shall by no means lose his reward.

These instructions should be what Christians expect when they are sent out to accomplish the work in the ministry of Jesus Christ, but many are unaware of the instructions or the conditions that are sure to happen.

Parables of the Kingdom (Matthew 13:1–52, Mark 4:1–20, 30–32, Luke 8:4–15, 13:20–21)

Every king has an operational plan for his kingdom. Jesus is no exception. Jesus is King of kings and Lord of lords; He has a plan of operation for His kingdom. These parables are a manual of operation with a specific plan for success of each principle. Each subject of the kingdom is expected to follow the plan if he or she expects to enjoy the kingdom's benefits. However, those who are not a part of the kingdom should not expect the kingdom's benefits. For that reason, Jesus uses parables giving a plain and general explanation of the kingdom's principles.

This sermon uses these parables to explain the operation of the kingdom. According to *Nelson's Illustrated Bible Dictionary,* a parable is a short, simple story designed to communicate a spiritual truth, religious principle, or moral lesson; a parable is also a figure of speech in which truth is illustrated by a comparison or example drawn from everyday experiences.

Jesus wanted this information to be clear and understandable because adhering to the rules of the kingdom would cause the subjects to have good success. The operation of the kingdom was indeed a mystery to all who were not subjects of the kingdom, and kingdom benefits were available only to those who were subjects. Therefore, Jesus explained in parables to enlighten the subjects and confound the non-subjects. Jesus explained His reason for using parables to His followers in Matthew 13:12–13, "For whosoever hath, to him shall be given, and he shall have more abundance: but whosoever hath not, from him shall be taken away even that he hath. Therefore speak I to them in parables: because they seeing see not; and hearing they hear not, neither do they understand."

Robert Farrar Capon, the author of *The Parables of the Kingdom,* mentions this in his book. The disciples wanted to know why Jesus taught in parables (riddles) rather than giving plain explanations. Capon gives the following explanation:

> Obligingly, Jesus tells them what the other subject is: the kingdom. (In Matthew, he calls it "the kingdom of heavens"; in Mark and Luke, "the kingdom of God"—but phrases are otherwise equivalent) "To you," he tells the disciples, "it is given to know the secrets [ta mysteria—the hidden things, the unobservable workings] of the kingdom, but for those outside, it is given only in parables."[10]

These parables were presented to a crowd on a beach; though everyone could hear, not everyone could understand. Jesus presented these kingdom operation principles as seven mysteries. Each one is explained as follows:

1. The Mystery of the Sower—This parable is also found in Mark 4:1–9 and in Luke 8:4–8. Jesus described this parable by using the farmer sowing seed and the yield on the seed based on the condition of the sowing. The farmer whom Jesus mentioned sowed the seeds in four different environments:

- Some seeds fell by the wayside, and the fowls came by and devoured them.
- Some seeds fell upon stony places where there was not much earth. The seed germinated and came up, but there was not a sufficient root system to sustain it when the sun came up. Therefore, the sun scorched the plant, and because it did not have sufficient roots it withered away.
- Some seeds fell among thorns, and the thorns sprang up and choked them.
- Some seeds fell on good ground and brought forth fruit. Some of the fruit brought forth a hundred times the seed sowed, some brought forth sixty times the seed sowed, and some brought forth thirty times the seed sowed.

Jesus explained also that many prophets and righteous men desired to know the secrets of the kingdom, but were not able to know them. Then Jesus went on to explain each situation of the seed sowing in Matthew 13:19–23: "When any one heareth the word of the kingdom, and understandeth it not, then cometh the wicked one, and catcheth away that which was sown in his heart. This is he which received seed by the way side. But he who received the seed into stony places, the same is he who heareth the word, and anon with joy receiveth it; Yet hath he not root in himself, but dureth for a while: for when tribulation or persecution ariseth because of the word, by and by he is offended. He also that received seed among the thorns is he that heareth the word; and the care of this world, and the deceitfulness of riches, choke the word, and he becometh unfruitful. But he that received seed into the good ground is he that heareth the word, and understandeth it; which also beareth fruit, and bringeth forth, some an hundredfold, some sixty, some thirty."

We note from this passage that the sower is God the Father, the seed is Jesus Christ the Son, and the earth is the people. Christians are to manifest fruit from the Word of God, which of course is Jesus Christ. Any area where the Word is received and followed will produce fruit because the Word works; it is fruitful. Therefore, when the Word is received in good ground it bears fruit thirty, sixty, or one hundred times what was received. However, the Enemy (Satan) also plants seeds. These seeds will grow and become thorns or weeds as we find in some of the following parables. Therefore, Christians should expect that there will be some thorns and weeds among them.

2. The Mystery of the Tares Among the Wheat—(A tare is a weed that grows in a grain field.) Jesus used this parable to explain the necessity for the kingdom dwellers to live in the same field as the non-kingdom dwellers. In the previous parable Jesus explained that God had sent the Word to all who would receive it. Some received the Word as good ground, and others did not; nevertheless, they had to grow together. Jesus prepared His followers to tolerate the tares by teaching them to be children of Him and their Father. We find this passage in Matthew 5:45, "That ye may be the children of your Father which is in heaven: for he maketh his sun to rise on the evil and on the good, and sendeth rain on the just and on the unjust." Perhaps some of the tares will accept Christ before it is too late. What is a better place to see Jesus than in the field with His followers? Jesus knows that the tares will have to be separated from the wheat, but we are not the ones to try to do the separation. He reserves that right for Himself, and at an appointed time He will judge and separate the two.

3. The Mystery of the Grain of Mustard Seed— Jesus explains the blessing of the gospel. Once the seed is planted, it grows beyond our ability to imagine and becomes great and significant. That phenomenal growth is truly a mystery in the natural world and in the spirit.

4. The Mystery of the Leaven—Jesus lets His followers know from this parable that the kingdom is as leaven—it has the ability to grow on its own. Jesus is saying that God provides the increase, and the operation of this increase is compared to the operation of leaven. Paul mentions to the Corinthians the problem of leaven (evil) contaminating the whole thing. The apostle Paul wrote in 1 Corinthians 5:6–8, "Your glorying is not good. Know ye not that a little leaven leaveneth the whole lump? Purge out therefore the old leaven, that ye may be a new lump, as ye are unleavened. For even Christ our passover is sacrificed for us: Therefore let us keep the feast, not with old leaven, neither with the leaven of malice and wickedness; but with the unleavened bread of sincerity and truth."

Jesus was telling them that hiding evil in the kingdom was dangerous because everything would be tainted by the evil that acted as leaven. The kingdom is designed to grow the things of God, which are all good; however, evil things will grow and change the character of the whole environment or situation. If Christians do not understand this parable, they will think that it is acceptable to harbor things like unforgiveness and still enjoy kingdom living.

5. The Mystery of the Hid Treasure—This parable explains the gospel truth of the inability to purchase salvation. The person in this parable is not able to obtain what the kingdom has to offer until he gives up all that he possesses.

6. The Mystery of the Pearl—Jesus used this parable to tell His followers that they cannot buy a position in the kingdom. Our Lord Jesus Christ has already paid the price. Nothing we have could cause us to be able to obtain so great a pearl as the kingdom of heaven. It's free. All that is needed is that a person be willing to give up the world and what it has to offer for salvation paid for by the blood of Jesus Christ.

7. The Mystery of the Drag Net—These parables are meant to explain the final judgment—the importance of understanding that all people will be in the net, but not all will be kept forever with the Lord. Some will remain, but others will be cast out. Capon describes this net as "one that is dragged through the water, indiscriminately taking in everything in its path, accordingly, the kingdom of heaven (and by extension, the church as the sacrament of that kingdom) manifests the same indiscriminateness. First reflection, therefore: As the net gathers up everything in its path—not only fish but also seaweed, flotsam, jetsam, and general marine debris—so too the kingdom gathers up everything in its path."[11]

Instructions to the Community (Matthew 18:1–35; Mark 9:33–37; Luke 9:46–48; Luke 15:3–7; Luke 17:3–4)

This is the sermon that Jesus used to explain to Christians how to operate in the community of believers. Jesus started this sermon by answering a question that the disciples put before Him. They asked Him, "Who is the greatest in the kingdom of heaven?" This question caused Him to preach a sermon. He began by calling a little child to sit in the midst of them, and He used the example of the presence and attitude of a child to explain His answer. He told them that all the subjects of the kingdom have the opportunity to be the greatest, but only those who humbled themselves as a little child will be able to do so.

Children are totally dependent on those in authority over them (usually their parents). In addition, the ones who are in authority over them are usually totally committed to them. Children are teachable and obedient to the authority over them. Children are generally loyal, trusting, unselfish, and unpretentious. They do not believe that the persons in authority over will harm them in any way; therefore, they have the will do anything asked and follow anywhere they are taken. This makes them very vulnerable to misuse and abuse by those over them who are not committed to their well-being or by those who do not love them.

Jesus gave this example of what it takes to be among the greatest in the kingdom of heaven. He told them they must be as "little children." He was not asking them to give up their natural adulthood, but to act as trusting children in the kingdom of heaven.

Now the disciples understood that this childlike attitude would cause them to also be very vulnerable. Jesus eased their minds by also letting it be known that anyone who received one of these little children received Him, and woe to anyone who offended one of these little children. He told them that offenses must come, but woe to the world because of offenses. After His warning that offenses must come, He also warned those who bring the offenses. He told them if their hand or foot offended, they should cut it off. It would be better not to have two hands or feet than to be cast into everlasting fire. He said the same for their eye. If they were to see an offense, it would be better for them to pluck out that eye rather than to be cast into hell fire.

Jesus continued with another warning, "Do not despise these little ones," because their angels always behold the face of His Father in heaven. Now Jesus' followers understood that He would take care of them in the vulnerability

45

of being as a little child. It becomes, therefore, a serious matter to bother a child of God in a negative way.

Jesus continued this sermon by explaining His position on the importance of the lost. He used an example of a shepherd looking for one lost sheep. He explained that a shepherd will look for a lost sheep until it is found because it is not the will of our Father that one of these little ones be lost.

Now that Jesus' followers understood that they are to be as little children, Jesus moved on to the next point of the problems that arise in relationships. This general attitude means seeking the good of others over good for yourself. What if your brother or sister does not follow Jesus' instructions concerning you and decides to trespass against you? What is to be done about those who abuse you and trespass against you? Jesus gave the following instructions:

- Go to your brother, just the two of you. If your brother hears, you have gained your brother.
- If your brother does not hear, you bring one or two witnesses so that every word may be established.
- If he still does not hear, take it to the church.
- If he ignores the church, let him be unto you as a heathen and a tax collector.

What you bind on earth will be bound in heaven, and what you loose on earth will be loosed in heaven. And if the two of you agree on earth as touching anything, it shall be done for you by our Father who is in heaven. For when two or three gather in Jesus' name, there He will be in the midst of them. Following this principle will cause Christians to be in unity and with one accord. This is a very critical element of kingdom living.

Do Christians follow Jesus' teaching today up to this point? Duncan Carr, the author of *Thirty-One Days In The Kingdom of God*, does not believe they do. He writes:

On the Day of Pentecost, the one hundred and twenty believers were "with one accord" when suddenly they were all filled with the Holy Spirit. The psalmist states that when brethren dwell together in unity it is like the precious oil upon the head, which is a representation of the anointing of the Holy Spirit. There does appear to be a link between unity and the anointing of the Holy Spirit from a power-filled ministry. Did not Jesus say, "Again I say to you that if two of you agree on earth concerning anything that they ask, it will be done for them by My Father in heaven. For where two or three are gathered together in My name, I am there in the midst of them" (Matt. 18:19–20)?

It is sad that there is so much criticism in the church, with one denomination condemning another's doctrine. If only we could all study the Word of God and see the truth and accept that there is not inconsistency or ambiguity on God's part. One church has accepted the truth that "if you confess with your mouth the Lord Jesus and believe in your heart that God has raised Him from the dead you will be saved" (Rom. 10:9). Another church quotes from Mark 16:16 that "He who believes and is baptized will be saved." Neither church accepts the other's plan of salvation. Brothers and sisters, the Word is consistent, and if we would only pray for God to give us wisdom (James 1:5), we would see that both scriptures are essentially saying the same things.[12]

After these directions, Peter asked a question: "How often should I forgive my brother that has sinned against me, seven times?" Jesus answered the question and continued the lesson by telling Peter to forgive seventy times seven times. Jesus went on to explain that forgiveness must be practiced if they want the Father in heaven to forgive them. Jesus knew of the tremendous sacrifice that He would make personally to redeem us all and save all who would believe from eternal death. If the Lord would do this for all of us, how much more should Christians forgive their trespassers? Jesus gave the example of a person who received tremendous forgiveness, but when the opportunity came for him to forgive, he refused. The fate of that person was to be delivered to the tormentors. Jesus told them that His Father would do the same unto them if they did not forgive every one of their brothers for their trespasses.

The Olivet Discourse (Matthew 24:1–25:46; Mark 13:1–37; Luke 21:5–36)

This last sermon preached by Jesus in the Book of Matthew starts with Jesus answering questions. The seed for the questions arose as Jesus was leaving the temple. His disciples came to Him and pointed out the greatness of the temple buildings. Jesus told them of the coming destruction of the temple and of Jerusalem. When they reached Mount Olivet they came to Him privately because they wanted to know when the temple would be destroyed. They asked Him the following questions:

- When will these things happen?
- What will be a sign of your coming and of the end of the world?

Jesus did not want His followers to be ignorant about the end of the ages (last things); therefore, He gave them information in this sermon regarding the end of the Old Testament, the New Testament, and the coming millennium age. The destruction of Jerusalem and the temple must have been hard to visualize and comprehend. Just as some thought Jesus' first coming meant taking control from the Romans, the disciples must have thought that Jesus would return after such vast destruction of the city and the temple. Jesus knew that the age of the New Testament would require that God's people no longer worship Him with animal sacrifices. He knew that He would be the sacrifice. Therefore, temple worship (with animal sacrifices), as they had known it in the Old Testament, had to cease. He also knew that the New Testament was not the end; therefore, He gave them information on all that was to come. All of this made this sermon difficult to understand, especially since Jesus communicated the answers to both of these questions, one mixed with the other.

Nelson's Illustrated Bible Dictionary agrees to a point and describes these questions and answers. Jesus' discussion on the Mount of Olives about the destruction of Jerusalem and the end of the world is in Matthew 24:1— 25:46, Mark 13:1–37, and Luke 21:5–36. Nelson writes that the disciples believed that the temple would be destroyed at the end of the world when, among other things, Jesus would return. Nelson gives this as the reason that Matthew records the two questions, "Tell us, when shall these things be? and what shall be the sign of your coming, and of the end of the world?" (Matt. 24:3). Nelson agrees that the Olivet discourse is difficult to understand because Jesus intermingles His answers to these two questions. But, it must be understood that Jesus wanted them to know what to expect before the destruction of the temple and of Jerusalem and what to expect concerning His return. Therefore, Jesus told them.

Nelson goes on to say that the key to unraveling Jesus' answers is the repetition of the key phrase "take heed" found in Mark 13:5, 13:23, 13:33. The first two-part question that they asked was, "Tell us, when shall these things be? and what shall be the sign when all these things shall be fulfilled?" (Mark 13:4). Jesus began by saying, "Take heed lest any man deceive you" (Mark 13:5). Then Jesus described the events leading up to the temple's destruction (vv. 6–22), and indeed these things happened as recorded by the historian Josephus and in a biblical account (the Book of Acts) about the personal experience of the apostles. For example, one of the events Jesus said would happen occurs in verse 9, "But take heed to yourselves: for they shall deliver you up to councils; and in the synagogues ye shall be beaten: and ye shall be brought before rulers and kings for my sake, for a testimony against them." These things did happen to the apostles, to some individually (as with Paul before Agrippa) and to others collectively (as with Peter and John before the Sanhedrin). Another example is found in verse 6, "For many shall come in my name, saying, I am Christ; and shall deceive many."

Alfred J. Church, the author of *The Story of the Last Days of Jerusalem*, the writings of Josephus, talks about this when the Romans recognized Vespasian and Titus as the Messiah. All of this happened during the Jewish revolt against the Romans. They were expecting the Messiah to help them accomplish this task. Since the majority of the Jewish nation did not receive Jesus as their Messiah, they continued to fight the Romans against all odds. Jesus warned those who believed in Him not to believe anyone else to be the "Christ" because others would come declaring to be the Messiah. Alfred Church wrote the following concerning this matter:

> They kept up the Messianic expectations of the people and hailed every step towards destruction as a step towards deliverance. Reports of comets, meteors, and all sorts of fearful omens and prodigies were interpreted as signs of the coming of the Messiah and his reign over the heathen. The Romans recognized the Messiah in Vespasian and Titus.[13]

In addition, the verses of Matthew 13:6–8 and 13:14–19 talk about wars and rumors of wars, nation against nation, earthquakes, famine, and troubles to be the beginnings of sorrows. Approximately seven years passed after the beginning of the Jewish revolt before the end came. They fought for seven years before the city (Jerusalem) was taken from them and the temple destroyed. This was the time that Jesus had warned them about.

Church confirms this when he writes about Palestine being a most unfortunate country in that time period. Israel, Church writes, brought upon itself unspeakable suffering and destruction. Jerusalem's final judgment is a part of eschatological (last things) discourses of Christ from a portion of this final sermon in Matthew. Jesus told them about the end long before the beginning.

Church writes the following statements from the historical account of Josephus concerning the prophecy that Jesus had given His followers:

51

The forbearance of God with his covenant people, who had crucified their own Savior, reached at last its limit. As many as could be saved in the usual way, were rescued. The mass of the people had obstinately set themselves against all improvement. James the Just, the man who was fitted, if any could be, to reconcile the Jews to the Christian religion, had been stoned by his hardened brethren, for whom he daily interceded in the temple; and with him the Christian community in Jerusalem had lost its importance for that city. The hour of the "great tribulation" and fearful judgment drew near. The prophecy of the Lord approached its literal fulfillment: Jerusalem was razed to the ground, the temple burned, and not one stone was left upon another.

Not long before the outbreak of the Jewish war, seven years before the siege of Jerusalem (AD 63), a peasant by the name of Joshua, or Jesus, appeared in the city at the Feast of Tabernacles, and in a tone of prophetic ecstasy cried day and night on the street among the people: A voice from the morning, a voice from the evening! A voice from the four winds! A voice of rain against Jerusalem and the Temple! A voice against the bridegrooms and the brides! A voice against the whole people! Woe, woe to Jerusalem!" The magistrates, terrified by this woe, had the prophet of evil taken up and scourged. He offered no resistance, and continued to cry his "Woe." Being brought before the procurator, Albinus, he was scourged till his bones could be seen, but interposed not a word for himself; uttered no curse on his enemies; simply exclaimed at every blow in a mournful tone: "Woe, woe to Jerusalem!" To the governor's question, who and whence he was, he answered nothing. Finally they let him go, as a madman. But he continued for seven years and five months, till the outbreak of the war, especially at the three great feasts, to proclaim the approaching fall of Jerusalem. During the siege he was singing his dirge, for the last time, from the wall. Suddenly he added: "Woe, woe also to me!"—and a stone of the Romans hurled at his head put an end to his prophetic lamentation.[14]

After giving the warnings, Jesus then said, "But take ye heed: behold, I have foretold you all things" (Mark 13:23). By repeating the phrase "all things," He provides a conclusion to the first answer.

Nelson continues to talk about this phase being the keynote in this first answer of the warning "take heed"; there will be persecutions (Mark 13:9–13), wars and famines (13:7–8), false prophets, and false messiahs (13:6), all of which will lead up to the destruction of Jerusalem (13:14–23). These have all been confirmed by historical accounts.

But Jesus told His followers that despite all these woes they must "take heed" because "the end shall not be yet" (Mark 13:7). Mark 13:6–23 is therefore the answer to the question of the time of the temple's destruction. Additionally, it is an accurate historical account of the devastation that existed in Jerusalem during the Roman siege in AD 70 when the city and the temple were finally destroyed. Jesus' prophecy was therefore fulfilled in the years leading up to the temple's destruction (although some would say it is also a picture of what will be fulfilled again at the end of time).

AD 70 was also approximately the time when the apostles and the other followers of Christ had evangelized the entire known world. According to the Book of Acts, the apostles Peter and Stephen ministered first in Jerusalem. Immediately after the death of Stephen the church began to experience severe persecution, and many of Jesus' followers left Jerusalem and began to minister in other parts of the world. The persecution caused the preaching of the gospel to transition to Samaria and Judea with the primary mission work done by Philip, Peter, and Saul at the beginning of Saul's ministry. The next expansion was to the uttermost part. This venture included the ministry of Barnabas; Paul's first, second, and third missionary journeys; and, finally, Paul's imprisonment in Jerusalem, Cesarea, and Rome. After Paul completed his three journeys, he was imprisoned for the last time AD 67 or AD 68, which is also the approximate time of his death.

This is a historical account of what happened, even to the point of how the people were running from the Romans with no time to pack their belongings to leave Jerusalem! There are also accounts of how pregnant women were cut open (a practice common to this ancient era), giving an indication of what is also to come. If in fact the Old Testament is the New Testament concealed and the New Testament is the the Old Testament revealed, then it is logical that the New Testament is the millennium concealed. Therefore, we can expect the end of the New Testament age to be according to the description that Jesus gave of the end of the Old Testament era.

Again Nelson reminds us that Jesus' followers believed that the temple would be destroyed only at the end of the world. In fact, what Jesus had in mind was that the temple worship would cease as they had known it, and the method of worshiping God would change. No longer would the priests be able to continue to worship God in the former way. Only the new order (the church) would be the proper way to gain salvation through belief and faith in the Lord Jesus Christ, His death, and His resurrection from the dead. The disciples were mistaken in their assumption that the temple would remain until the return of the Lord Jesus Christ. Jesus told them that despite all the woes leading up to the temple's destruction, when it happened the end of the world still would not be in sight.

Therefore, in Mark 13:24–27 He answered their next logical question: What signs will precede the end of the world? The phrase in those days is a common Old Testament expression used when speaking of the end times. In those days there will be signs in the heavens, such as lightning coming out of the east and shining even unto the west, and then Jesus, the Son of Man, will come. In addition, immediately after the tribulations of those days, the sun will darken and the moon will not give light (notice that this is what happened at Jesus' crucifixion and resurrection, and it is going to happen again). Jesus continued by saying that the stars will fall from heaven and the powers of heavens will be shaken, and then will appear the sign of the Son of Man in heaven. After this, all the tribes of the earth will mourn, and they will see the Son of Man coming in the clouds of heaven with power and great glory (this is what happened on His ascension, and it is going to happen again), and then Jesus will send His angels with a great sound of the trumpet, and they will gather together His elect from the four winds, from one end of heaven to the other. (This event has already happened in the Old Testament as the Feast of Trumpets. At the time of this feast, the priest would sound the trumpet, and all the people of God would stop what they were doing and come immediately to the temple. It did not matter what was going on; they stopped, whether in the field working or in the house. This is going to happen again as the calling of God's people.) This is the great gathering of the Church before the Lord's return.

Jesus goes on to tell them how it will happen. He tells them that it will be as it was in the days of Noah, when people went on with their daily business, not really paying attention to the signs. He tells them that no one will know the exact hour; therefore, two people will be working in the field together, and one will be taken and one will be left. Christians must therefore be ready when the trumpet sounds.

The New Unger's Bible Dictionary reports this Old Testament event as the Feast of Trumpets found in Leviticus 23:23–25, which speaks of the re-gathering of Israel to its homeland after the out-gathering of the church. Matthew 24:31 speaks of the Son of Man at His second advent, sending His angels with a great sound of a trumpet to gather together His elect (of Israel) from the four winds, from one end of heaven to the other.

Jesus told them that they must be prepared for His coming and must not be taken by surprise. Mark's gospel also mentions Jesus' remarks that no one except the Father knows exactly when "that day"—Christ's return at the end of time—will be. Therefore, Jesus warns them to be on guard by always being prepared for His return. After this, Jesus tells them how to be ready. He goes back to the kingdom of heaven and compares it to the story of the ten virgins. Five of them were wise and kept oil in their lamp ready for the return of the bridegroom, but five were foolish and were not prepared and waited until they heard the bridegroom coming before they began to prepare. Jesus, the bridegroom, warned them about waiting until the last minute to prepare because it will be too late, which the five foolish virgins found out. When they went to prepare, the bridegroom had left and the door was closed. When they came later to get in, Jesus told them, I know you not. This is an indication of the personal relationship that is needed with the bridegroom and the anointing that comes from such a relationship.

Jesus closed this sermon with an additional parable about the nature of the kingdom of heaven. This last parable presents the principle of using what is given to bring an increase. For this He used the parable of a master giving each of three servants five, two, and one talent according to their ability. The one who had received five gained another five, and the one who received two gained another two, and to each of these the master said, "Well done. You are a good and faithful servant, you have been faithful over a few things, and I will make you ruler over many things. Now enter into the joy of your lord." But the one who received one talent hid it and did not get any gain from what he had been given. Not only did he not gather any gain, but he tried to justify himself by saying that he did not do so because his master was a man who reaped where he had not sown and gathered where he had not worked. The master said unto that one, "You wicked and slothful servant; you knew all of that when I gave you the talent. Why did you not put my money in the bank so that I could receive some gain from it?" The master then took the talent from him and gave it to the one who had ten talents, then cast the person who had not gained from the one talent into outer darkness. By this example Jesus let His followers know that each one would be given talents and gifts, and they were all expected to go out and increase. After all was said and done, Jesus presented Himself as the King who will separate the nations and put the sheep on His right hand and the goats on His left hand. He will give the sheep the kingdom prepared for them by His Father from the foundation of the world. For He commends them for feeding Him when he was hungry, giving Him water when He was thirsty, taking Him in when He was a stranger, and visiting Him when He was in prison.

The sheep wanted to know, "When did we do all this?" and He answered, "When you did this for the least of my brothers, you did it for me." Then He spoke to the goats on his left and sent them away to everlasting fire that has been prepared for the Devil and his angels. Now the followers understood what they must do. After all five of the sermons, Jesus concluded with these statements. They also knew that they could not be selfish and ignore all the previous teaching. They will not be able to explain this type of behavior. Jesus had commanded His followers to love one another and put others before their personal wants. He had promised to take care of their needs, but He expected them to share with one another, so that none would suffer need.

In addition, He told them to be kind to widows, the fatherless, and strangers. Jesus told the goats that they did not feed the hungry, they did not clothe the naked, they did not take care of the sick, nor did they visit the prisoners; therefore, they would experience everlasting punishment, and the righteous would experience eternal life.

All of these sermons represent Christian instructions for living a kingdom lifestyle. Does the church universally take care of widows and the fatherless? There is not much evidence of such activities thriving in the church today as reported in the research material gathered for this book.

Obedience to these instructions would cause each Christian to live a victorious life saved from many of the perils and problems that come to pass because of disobedience. Each of these instructions has a kingdom blessing intended for Christian living. These instructions also have a side intended for non-Christians. The good news about all of the commandments that Jesus taught is that they are designed to improve the quality of life here on earth and the advancement the kingdom. The success of Christians in their daily living depends on their understanding the rules of the kingdom and the consequences of not following the rules.

The kingdom's blessing and benefits are not intended for non-believers of the Lord Jesus Christ. Some of them wanted to justify their desire to stay under the Old Testament covenant by asking Jesus tricky questions. One such person, a lawyer mentioned in Matthew 22:35–40, tempted him, asking, "Master, which is the great commandment in the law?" Jesus said unto him, "Thou shalt love the Lord thy God with all thy heart, and with all thy soul, and with all thy mind. This is the first and great commandment. And the second is like unto it, Thou shalt love thy neighbor as thyself. On these two commandments hang all the law and the prophets." They did not believe Him, or else they would not have tried to trick Him. If they had believed, then they could have known the secrets of the kingdom. If Christians obey these two commandments, they will have obeyed all of the commands of the kingdom. There is no way to obey these two commandments and not be in line with what Jesus taught in the five sermons under review in this study.

Many Christians say that we are now living in the New Testament times, and we are not under the Old Testament law; therefore, we do not have to follow the Ten Commandments of Moses because they are recorded in the Old Testament. All of these commandments, with the exception of the Sabbath Day, are mentioned in the New Testament gospels; however, knowing and living are two different things. Jesus taught them how to live by His Word. That is what these five sermons are all about. One example is the command to love your neighbor. Jesus knew the heart of the Father concerning this command. The Good Samaritan is a good example of the command. The command to love your enemies is another. Jesus Himself loved His enemies; He asked the Father to forgive those who nailed him to the cross and all the others that abused and misused Him. Everything that He commanded His followers to do He did before He left the earth. After each of these sermons, Jesus taught His disciples how to apply what He had just taught. We will review some of these activities in the next chapter.

Many Christians say, "I want to be like Jesus," but they don't really understand what they are saying. If they did, there would be less whining and murmuring over persecution and personal attacks and more tolerance and understanding of those who labor among them.

From all of this Jesus made it plain that God is the Father of all, and none of His children can come to Him wanting to destroy any of His other children because of their personal needs, wants, habits, and intolerances. Christians should know how much God loves sinners, not to mention their sisters and brothers. Without such love they are not going to be able to enjoy the fullness of the benefits of kingdom living if they refuse to forgive and obey God. Christians are not going to be able to complain to God and seek revenge on their sisters or brothers. What good parent would allow such activity in the family structure? Not one! God will not allow it either. It is not the desire of the Lord that one should be lost. It is also not His desire that any of His followers be abuse or misused; they are His little children.

CHAPTER 3

DO CHRISTIANS OBEY THE
CHRISTIAN TORAH?

How the Church Has Taught Obedience to the Christian Torah

Jesus gave very specific instructions in each of His five sermons. All instructions from these sermons clearly indicate a change of outward expression of worship to inward worship from the heart based upon the love of God and of our neighbors. The results of this relationship will manifest an outward expression of love that comes from the heart and is demonstrated in many unselfish ways.

Jesus' demonstration of love is second to none. Jesus has not asked most Christians to die physically for the sake of the Gospel. Some have that assignment, but most do not. Jesus only asked most to die to the flesh. It really takes dying to the flesh in order to love God and people as He commands Christians to do.

The early church (first century) followed the commands of Jesus just as He taught them. The apostles who walked with Him taught the commands, and the early church followed the teaching. Acts 2:42–47 confirms this practice. According to verse 42, they continued steadfastly in the apostles' doctrine and fellowship, in breaking of bread, and in prayers. This passage goes on to say that they had all things in common. They sold their possessions and goods and shared with everyone in need. And continuing daily with one accord in the temple, and breaking bread from house to house, they did eat their meat with gladness and singleness of heart, praising God and having favor with all the people. And the Lord added to the church daily those who should be saved. The apostles, especially the apostle Paul, were constantly teaching the Christian Torah. As mentioned earlier, love is the key to being able to do all that Christ commands Christians to do. This truth is evidenced by the Word given to the Corinthians. In 1 Corinthians 13, the apostle Paul taught them about the nature of love. Practicing love is not easy. It requires suffering, commitment, sacrifice, service, and understanding. In addition, the apostle Paul taught love according to the categories mentioned in each of the five sermons. How are Christians able to line up their lives according to the Christian Torah? Love is the answer. Paul taught that love manifests itself in Christian relationships first to God, then to people, to oneself, and finally to the community of believers and the community at large. These categories are mentioned in the *Word In Life Study Bible* as follows:[15]

1. Love and Oneself (1 Cor. 13:4)—"Charity suffereth long, and is kind; charity envieth not; charity vaunteth not itself, is not puffed up."

- **Love does not rival for attention (envy).** Jesus taught that Christians must not put themselves first. Remember, He said if someone forces you to go one mile, go with him or her two miles.
- **Love does not brag on itself (parade).** Jesus taught that Christians should pray in secret and not try to get recognition from men, nor should they give alms before men to be seen of them, otherwise they have no reward from our Father in heaven.

- **Love does not inflate itself (puff up).** Jesus taught, "Blessed are the meek, for they shall inherit the earth."

2. Love and Relationships (1 Cor. 13:5) —"Doth not behave itself unseemly, seeketh not her own, is not easily provoked, thinketh no evil."

- **Love does not tread on others' feelings (act rude).** Jesus taught you to love your enemies, bless them that curse you, and do good to them that hate you.
- **Love does not take another's things (seek its own).** Jesus taught that if any man will sue you with the law and take away your coat, let him also have your cloak.
- **Love does not offend easily (become provoked).** Jesus taught that whoever is angry with his brother without a cause shall be in danger of judgment.

3. Love and Sin (1 Cor. 13:6)—"Rejoiceth not in iniquity, but rejoiceth in the truth."

- **Love does not keep a record of wrongs suffered (no evil).** Jesus taught, "Blessed are ye when men shall revile you, and persecute you, and shall say all manner of evil against you falsely, for my sake. Rejoice, and be exceedingly glad: for great is your reward in heaven." (Matt. 5:11-12)
- **Love does not make unrighteousness its object of rejoicing (rejoice in iniquity).** Jesus also taught, "Blessed are they that mourn: for they shall be comforted." (Matt. 5:4)
- **Love celebrates others' achievements in right-eousness (rejoices in the truth).** Jesus taught that Christians are all one in Him. Therefore, when one

is in need, all are; when one is happy, all are; and when one is sad, all are.

4. Love and Others (1 Cor. 13:7)—"Beareth all things, believeth all things, hopeth all things, endureth all things"

- **Love keeps all things in confidence (bears all things).** Jesus taught that Christians will be persecuted for His name's sake. He warned His followers in Matthew 10:17, "But beware of men: for they will deliver you up to the councils, and they will scourge you in their synagogues." But Christians must still love their persecutors because that is exactly what He did for Christians on the cross.

- **Love knows what God can do (believes all things).** Jesus taught this subject with the fig tree situation in Mark 11:21–22. "And Peter calling to remembrance saith unto Him, Master, behold, the fig tree which thou cursedst is withered away. And Jesus answering saith unto them, Have faith in God." Therefore, believe all things; have faith in God.

- **Love holds out holy ambitions for others to achieve (hopes all things).** Jesus taught His followers to have faith in Him, for it is impossible to please Him without faith. Faith is the substance of things hoped for, the evidence of things not seen (Heb. 11:1). Therefore, hope for all things.

- **Love survives under every condition (endures all things).** Jesus taught by His own example that Christians are to love people regardless of the situation and circumstances around them. We do not fight with people but with principalities and powers.

The early church practiced all that Jesus taught them. When there was misunderstanding and misinformation among them, the apostles gave them the understanding and the information they needed to know what to do and how to act.

Christians today have a greater challenge. They are not necessarily taught the commands that Jesus left them. Sometimes Christians forget that Jesus is the Shepherd and the Lamb (sacrifice) or that He is King, Lord, and servant. Therefore, it may be possible for them to see themselves as shepherds and not as sacrificial lambs (living sacrifices), or for them to see themselves as kings and lords but not necessarily as servants. This type of imbalance may cause some Christians not to see the lost as the Lord sees them. One reality check that is good to remember is that Jesus loves sinners. He loves sinners with a passion! Some Christians think that He does not like them because they are sinners. If you ask them, they will tell you that they know that they were once lost and saved by grace. But when they are confronted with others who are where they used to be, they don't seem to have much patience or tolerance for those who have not yet become a part of the faith.

One common problem that displays this truth is the fact that many Christians expect unsaved people to act like saved people, and when they do not, they get angry or they decide to write them off as lost causes. But Jesus died for all of His creations; therefore, it is not possible for a person to be too sinful for His love to reach them. This (love God, love people, and put others first) is basic in following Jesus' commands to Christians in these five sermons under study. This type of behavior will cause sinners to see the love of Christ.

Following the teaching of Christ is not new to Christians of today. However, over the many years of church history, the revelation of the following and obeying the commands of Christ does surface from time to time. One example is the ministry of John Wesley (1703–91), the founder of the Methodist Church. Reverend Wesley believed that Christians should follow the ordinances of the Lord Jesus Christ. He believed that Christians should grow up with the help of the Holy Spirit into the perfected man.

Reverend Wesley knew that none of us can attain perfection; we are all flesh and blood. However, we can grow up in the things of God, and that is precisely what Reverend Wesley was talking about. The perfections that Reverend Wesley was talking about are from the sanctification process after salvation. He talks about perfection as it relates to maturity in Christ. The perfect man is not new according to the teaching of Reverend Wesley. The Book of Job (Job 8:20) mentions that God will not cast away a perfect man. Psalm 37:37 mentions that the perfect man's end is peace. James 2:3 mentions that a man who offends not in word is a perfect man. The apostle Paul writes to the Ephesian Church, in Ephesians 4:13, about coming unto a perfect man, and Jesus Himself speaks about this in the Sermon on the Mount (Matthew 5:48), "Be ye therefore perfect, even as your Father which is in heaven is perfect."

Reverend Wesley goes on to explain that a person who is perfect is one who has the mind of Christ inside himself, walks as Christ walked, has clean hands and a pure heart, is cleansed from all filthiness of flesh and spirit, and does not stumble or commit sin. Reverend Wesley talked about understanding the scriptural expression "a perfect man" as one in whom God has fulfilled His faithful word; who has no filthiness; whom God has sanctified throughout in body, soul, and spirit; and who walks in the light and not darkness, the blood of Jesus Christ His Son having cleansed him from all sin. Therefore, this man can now testify to all mankind, "I am crucified with Christ: nevertheless, I live; yet not I, but Christ lives in me." He is holy as God who called him is holy, both in heart and in all manner of conversation. He loves the Lord His God with all his heart and serves Him with all of his strength. He loves his neighbor, every man as himself, as Christ loves us, especially those who persecute him because they know not the Son or the Father. Indeed his soul is all love, filled with mercies, kindness, meekness, gentleness, and longsuffering. His life agrees with what he is, and whatever he does, he does in the name of the Lord Jesus Christ.

Reverend Wesley preached many great sermons from the teachings of Jesus. (This information regarding the preaching and teaching of Reverend Wesley was taken from sermon 16 of the 1872 edition.) The Sermon on the Mount is one in particular that he used to edify and encourage Christians to follow the teaching of Christ in order to work out their souls' salvation in striving to become the perfect man and become mature in the things of God as Christ intended. Reverend Wesley's common thread in this teaching is love. If you are following all of the commands of Jesus Christ and not motivated by love, then it is all for nothing.

How We Can Determine Our Obedience to the Christian Torah

Are Christians today learning the instructions (ordinances) of Jesus that are found in the Christian Torah? There are several ways to acquire the information found in the Christian Torah. The most common way is to examine preaching at church on Sunday mornings; however, the teachings can also be taught in weekly Bible studies, in special Bible classes, in television and radio programs, and in literature. The best way to find out if Christians are learning these instructions is to ask some of them. We can also

67

search the literature and find out what is being written on the subject. This section is focused on the availability of Christian literature on this subject.

Some Christians believe that these instructions are not for Christians today but for future generations or for those who will be here during the millennium dispensation. Either one of these positions makes it easier for Christians to be complacent about conforming to what Jesus wanted His followers to do. The literature on the subject generally does not support either of those positions. There are many authors who write and teach today's application of one or more of the sermons that are included in the Christian Torah. This section includes some of the writing and teaching of such authors.

According to Bill Dodds and Michael J. Dodds, the authors of *Happily Ever After Begins Here and Now: Living the Beatitudes Today*,[16] the problem with saying, "I am a Christian" is that it gives the impression that following Christ is a state of being. In their discussion regarding Matthew 5:9, "Blessed are the peacemakers: for they shall be called the children of God," they say that following Christ is not a state of being, but a series of actions. Jesus is telling people, "If you take this action, then the reactions will be your position in God's family." This is an action. This beatitude is not about being at peace; it is about making peace happen. Dodds and Dodds go on to say that the peace that Jesus is talking about is true peace, not false peace. The difference between true and false peace is the difference between evil peace and good peace. Evil peace can happen when evil makes an agreement with evil to cooperate and to call a truce for a time. For instance, honor among thieves is based on fear and expediency, while true peace is based on the integrity of our relationship with God.

We make the choice to become more like our Creator, and one of the ways to do that is by becoming a person who makes peace. People sometimes say, "There is nothing like having peace." Having peace is good, but it is also good to be called a child of God.

Arthur W. Pink, the author of *An Exposition of the Sermon on the Mount,*[17] encourages Christians to earnestly seek grace to strive to be more than just astonished with this sermon, namely receive it into our hearts and minds and incorporate it into our daily walk.

Sinclair B. Ferguson, the author of *The Sermon on the Mount,*[18] speaks to leaders in his book. He writes, "Those of us who teach or preach would do well to study these and other elements in our Lord's ministry, and to give time to examining how faithful our own approach to the teaching is to that of our Lord and Master Jesus Christ. If we do this we bear rich and lasting fruit in our Christian service."

Warren W. Wiersbe, the author of *Live Like a King— Developing a Royal Lifestyle from the Beatitudes,*[19] writes that Christians are never finished with the Beatitudes. There are many new things to be found in our hearts as we grow in grace. As we do that, we also grow in the knowledge of Christ and of ourselves. Wiersbe is specifically speaking about Christians being salt and light. With that in mind, he reminds Christians that there is always new territory in our lives to conquer and control. Therefore, we enjoy the kingdom that we might enlarge the kingdom.

In addition to the comments of the above authors, Pat Robertson, the author of *The Secret Kingdom—Your Path to Peace, Love, and Financial Security,* discusses the laws associated with the instructions that Jesus left us in the Christian Torah. Robertson calls these laws the "laws of the kingdom." Jesus makes simple declarations that reveal these laws. One such statement is, "Give and it shall be given to you." Robertson writes that these words form a spiritual principle that touches every relationship, every condition of man, whether spiritual or physical. Robertson gave the following examples of the spiritual laws and the associated benefits of each:[20]

- The Law of Reciprocity—Give and it shall be given unto you.
- The Law of Use—Use it and multiply it, or lose it.
- The Law of Perseverance—If we keep on knocking, the door will open; if we keep on seeking we shall find; and if we keep on asking, it shall be given.
- The Law of Responsibility—Those who have been given much must know that much is required from God and man. We are expected to perform well in whatever opportunity is given to us. If we perform well, we will be given more to do, plus favor.
- The Law of Greatness—The greatest person in the kingdom of heaven is the one who makes himself humble like a child and a servant of all.
- The Law of Unity—God's power is released when unity is present.
- The Law of Fidelity—Whoever can be trusted with a very little can be trusted with much.
- The Law of Change—No one should put new wine into an old wine skin, or it will break and the wine will be lost.
- The Law of Miracles—God is willing to disrupt the natural order of things in order to accomplish His purpose. We must take our eyes off what we see and focus on what we do not see, having faith with-

out doubting and speaking about those things as though they were.

- The Law of Dominion—As Christians we have regained our position of having dominion. In other words, we are to rule over the earth as kings and lords.

Robertson goes on to say that putting this together with the world's greatest teaching that love is at the heart of God's will establishes the perfect "law" for conduct: "You shall love your neighbor as yourself." In addition, Robertson defines the "Law of Reciprocity," the first law mentioned above, as a kingdom principle revealed in these teachings of the Lord. It is relatively easy to identify since it is visible in various Bible chapters that contain these sermons. The basic law of physics says that for every action there is an equal and opposite reaction. The jet and space age in which we live was founded on this law, and so is the teaching of our Lord Jesus Christ.

Christians today are affected by these laws whether they know them are not. Christians can no longer hide their heads in the sand and pretend that the choices that they make yield only positive results. Jesus meant for Christians to experience only the best because He always gave the blessing for obedience and the negative consequences for disobedience.

Jesus wants His followers to consistently obey His commands. Then they shall have great success. Otherwise, they may find themselves walking down a dangerous path. Edwin K. Broadhead, the author of *The Sermon on the Mount—Demand and Grace,* talks about the principle of consistency[21] (Matt. 7:15–23). He mentions that the kingdom originates with God's availability, and it must be marked by the disciple's consistency. He goes on to say that the hardest criticism that Jesus had against the religious leaders was the fact that they did not practice what they preached. Their values were inconsistent with their lifestyle. Jesus labeled these folks as hypocrites. The Book of Matthew warns the Christian community about this danger for such leaders because they are labeled as false prophets and compared to wolves in sheep's clothing. This danger continues today and is still valid. For this reason, Christians must be consistent in following the teachings of Jesus.

Examples are given of the tree and the kind of fruit it produces, the connection between words and lifestyle. The kingdom of God is not about busy religious activity; it is about transformed lives that confess Jesus' lordship through words and deeds and a willingness to follow Him and obey His commands.

A Real-Life Study of Christians' Obedience to the Christian Torah

As stated earlier, the best way to find out if Christians are learning these instructions is to ask some of them. The remainder of this book focuses on a survey questionnaire that was prepared with questions based on each of the five sermons under study and general questions that provided information about the source of the information that had been taught, preached, or obtained through personal study. The questions represented the moral and spiritual instructions given to Christians in order to live the abundant life that Jesus desires for each. These instructions give Christians direction concerning living in the kingdom of God and how to be in relationship with God, with each other, with the community, and in business and personal activities.

The questionnaire was designed to determine the following from each participant:

- The participant's general knowledge of each sermon
- The participant's source of the general knowledge (preaching, teaching, or personal study)
- The participant's understanding of each sermon as it relates to relationship with God, self, family, believers, community, and business.
- The participant's reasons for knowing or not knowing the details of each sermon
- The participant's personal knowledge of the details of each sermon
- The participant's personal study of each sermon
- The participant's use of the knowledge of these sermons in daily living

The persons surveyed were all Christians. Among the persons surveyed were Christian educators, pastors, teachers (Christian and secular), children (old enough to understand), writers, students, business owners, employees of various government and private organizations, ministers, deacons, and elders. Both male and female respondents participated. The results represent a limited sample of people from all walks of life. Therefore, the findings represent this limited sample of believers.

The next chapter discusses the findings from the survey. The first chart that presents the sermon knowledge results provides some interesting information regarding the survey participants. The survey questionnaire was divided into seven sections. Each of the first five sections asked questions regarding the ordinances commanded by Jesus specific to that particular sermon. Section six collected data about personal familiarity with each sermon. The seventh section collected data regarding the method by which the individuals acquired the information about each sermon and data regarding the reasons for not having been exposed to the information. There was also a section in the last part of the survey that allowed for comments and personal observations of the individual sermons or general comments regarding spiritual growth in this arena. Many participants were thankful that the importance of knowing what Jesus taught Himself had been brought to their attention through this survey, and others were interested in understanding the analysis and results.

CHAPTER 4

A SURVEY OF CHRISTIANS' KNOWLEDGE AND OBEDIENCE

The following chart represents the data findings of the Sermon Obedience Results:

SERMON OBEDIENCE RESULTS

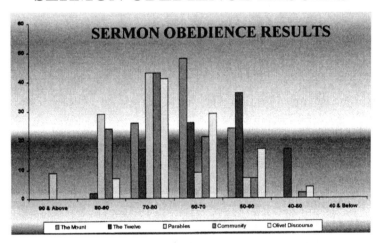

Notice the Sermon Obedience Results chart. The scoring of the sermons was based upon the percentage of the questions answered according to what Jesus commanded Christians to do. The overall score is the final score for each sermon, and it was derived from a percentage of questions answered correctly.

The data from the questionnaire provides the following information gathered for each sermon (the ranking of each sermon is by numbers with one (1) being the highest).

The sermon that is 90% and above adhered to by the survey participants:
1. Parables of the Kingdom

The Parables of the Kingdom sermon is the only sermon with participants scoring high enough to adhere to 90% of the commands that Jesus directed. As mentioned earlier, this sermon talks about the mysteries of the sower who sowed seed on different types of ground, the tares among the wheat, the grain of mustard seed's yielding phenomenal growth, the danger of leaven, the great treasure of a fertile field, the great pearl, and the drag net. These parables are well known, but the high percentage of the practice of the principle is surprising because the Sermon on the Mount is the one that the participants know best. The Sermon on the Mount is mentioned in detail in chapter two. It is the sermon that Jesus used to describe the personal characteristics and behavior of Christians.

The sermons that are 80% but less than 90% adhered to by the survey participants:
1. Parables of the Kingdom
2. Instructions to the Community
3. The Olivet Discourse
4. Instructions to the Twelve

The highest-ranking sermon in this category is also "Parables of the Kingdom." Eighty percent of the time, the participants obeyed the principles preached in this sermon. It seems that the participants were more willing to obey Jesus in these parable situations than any of the others. This is the first appearance of Instructions to the Community, and it is the second most adhered-to sermon. This is the sermon in which Jesus taught the conditions for entering the kingdom of heaven as being converted and coming into the kingdom as a little child. The third most adhered-to sermon is the Olivet Discourse. The Olivet Discourse is the sermon that Jesus used to explain the end of the age and His return. The fourth most adhered-to sermon in this category is the Instructions to the Twelve; this is the sermon that Jesus used to give instructions to those whom He sent out to find the lost sheep and bring them into the fold. The survey participants seem to be more willing to change others than themselves.

The sermons that are 70% but less than 80% adhered to by the survey participants:
1. The Parables of the Kingdom and Instructions to the Community
2. The Olivet Discourse
3. The Sermon on the Mount
4. Instructions to the Twelve

Seventy percent of the participants obeyed the "Parables of the Kingdom" and "The Instructions to the Community." These two sermons tied at this level of obedience. "The Olivet Discourse" ranked second in this category. This is also surprising since this is the sermon that the participants have the least knowledge of.

The sermons that are 60% but less than 70% adhered to by the survey participants:
1. The Sermon on the Mount
2. The Olivet Discourse
3. Instructions to the Twelve

4. Instructions to the Community
5. Parables of the Kingdom

The participants obeyed the instructions of the "The Sermon on the Mount" 60% of the time. This is the sermon that they all reported having the most knowledge of.

The sermons that are 50% but less than 60% adhered to by the survey participants:
1. Instructions to the Twelve
2. The Sermon on the Mount
3. The Olivet Discourse
4. Parables of the Kingdom and Instructions to the Community

Fifty percent of the time the participants obeyed the above sermons in the order of the above list.

The sermons that are 40% but less than 50% adhered to by the survey participants:
1. Instructions to the Twelve
2. The Olivet Discourse
3. Instructions to the Community

Some of the participants reported that they obeyed the above list 40% of the time.

The sermons that are 40% or below adhered to by the survey participants: None.

KNOWLEDGE RESULTS

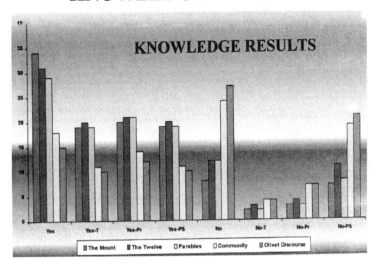

The chart above indicates the participants' knowledge of each sermon and the source. It also indicates the degree of not having knowledge and the possible reasons for not knowing about any particular sermon. The data from the questionnaire provides this information about each sermon (the ranking of each sermon is by numbers, with one (1) being the highest).

The sermon that survey participants had the most knowledge of:
1. The Sermon on the Mount
2. Instructions to the Twelve
3. Parables of the Kingdom
4. Instructions to the Community
5. The Olivet Discourse

The sermon that survey participants studied most often:
1. The Instructions to the Twelve
2. Parables of the Kingdom

3. The Sermon on the Mount
4. Instructions to the Community
5. The Olivet Discourse

The sermon that survey participants heard preached most often:

1. The Instructions to the Twelve and Parables of the Kingdom
2. The Sermon on the Mount
3. Instructions to the Community
4. The Olivet Discourse

The sermon that survey participants heard taught most often:

1. The Instructions to the Twelve
2. The Sermon on the Mount and Parables of the Kingdom
3. Instructions to the Community
4. The Olivet Discourse

The sermon on which the survey participants received little or no preaching:

1. Instructions to the Community and The Olivet Discourse
2. Instructions to the Twelve
3. The Sermon on the Mount and Parables of the Kingdom

The sermon on which survey participants received little or no teaching:

1. Instructions to the Community and The Olivet Discourse
2. Instructions to the Twelve
3. The Sermon on the Mount and Parables of the Kingdom

The sermon in which survey participants invested little or no personal study time:

1. The Olivet Discourse
2. Instructions to the Community
3. Instructions to the Twelve
4. Parables of the Kingdom
5. The Sermon on the Mount

Jesus wanted His followers to obey Him not just because He is God, Lord, and King, but because of the great benefits, the love attached to each command, and the joy of each promise. In His first dealings with His people going into the land that He had promised them, God told them to obey His commands and gave them the reasons for His request.

Moses taught the people in Deuteronomy 6:24–25, "And the LORD commanded us to do all these statutes, to fear the LORD our God, for our good always, that He might preserve us alive, as it is at this day. And it shall be our righteousness, if we observe to do all these commandments before the LORD our God, as he hath commanded us."

We notice from this passage that the obedience request was for the good of the people and was not meant for evil. God gave them good news regarding how they would be blessed because of their obedience. We find this in Deuteronomy 7:11–25, where the LORD commanded them to keep His commandments. In verse 11 He says, "Thou shalt therefore keep the commandments, and the statutes, and the judgments, which I command thee this day, to do them."

The LORD goes on to tell them that if they listen to these judgments and keep them, He will do the following:

- The LORD thy God shall keep unto thee the covenant and the mercy which He swear unto thy fathers.

- And He will love thee, and bless thee, and multiply thee.
- He will also bless the fruit of thy womb and the fruit of thy land, thy corn, thy wine, thine oil, the increase of thy kind, and the flocks of thy sheep in the land which He sware unto thy fathers to give thee.
- Thou shalt be blessed above all people: there shall not be male or female barren among you, or among your cattle.
- And the LORD will take away from thee all sickness, and will put none of the evil diseases of Egypt, which thou knowest, upon thee, but will lay them upon all them that hate thee.
- And thou shalt consume all the people which the LORD thy God shall deliver thee; thine eye shall have no pity upon them: neither shalt thou serve their gods; for that will be a snare unto thee.
- If thou shalt say in thine heart, these nations are more than I; how can I dispossess them? Thou shalt not be afraid of them: but shalt well remember what the LORD thy God did unto Pharaoh, and unto all Egypt.
- The great temptations which thine eyes saw, and the signs, and the wonders, and the mighty hand, and the stretched out arm, whereby the LORD thy God brought thee out: so shall the LORD thy God do unto all the people of whom thou art afraid.
- Moreover the LORD thy God will send the hornet among them, until they that are left, and hide themselves from thee, be destroyed.
- Thou shalt not be affrighted at them: for the LORD thy God is among you, a mighty God and terrible.

- And the LORD thy God will put out those nations before thee by little and little: thou mayest not consume them at once, lest the beasts of the field increase upon thee.
- But the LORD thy God shall deliver them unto thee, and shall destroy them with a mighty destruction, until they be destroyed.
- And He shall deliver their kings into thine hand, and thou shalt destroy their name from under heaven: there shall no man be able to stand before thee, until thou hast destroyed them.

All of this sounds wonderful in the Old Testament, but what can we expect in the New Testament? The same is true for Christians today. We see the LORD GOD doing the same thing in the New Testament. In Matthew 17:1–5, Mark 9:7, and Luke 9:28–36, Peter, James, and John went with Jesus up a high mountain, and while they were there, Jesus was transfigured before them. During the time of the transfiguration, a cloud overshadowed them, and a voice came out of the cloud, saying, "This is my beloved Son: hear him." The word "hear" in this sentence is not just hearing with the natural ear. It is a Greek word akouo (ak-oo'-o) that means to understand, to comprehend, to be familiar with, or to know.

There were many instances where the importance of obedience was demonstrated. Jesus showed His followers that all that He had created obeyed Him. This is seen in Matthew 8:27 when men marveled because the winds and the sea obeyed Him! It is seen in Mark 1:27 when they were all amazed that the unclean spirits obeyed Him. How much more should man obey the Lord?

In Acts 5:29, when Peter and the other apostles were confronted with the command of men to obey them, they answered and said, "We ought to obey God rather than men." The apostle Paul told the people that they needed to obey the Epistle he had written. We find that in 2 Thessalonians 3:14: "And if any man obey not our word by this epistle, note that man, and have no company with him, that he may be ashamed." Christians all admit that they are children of God; therefore, God is their parent. In that case, Ephesians 6:1 says, "Children, obey your parents in the Lord: for this is right," applying to children in the natural world as well as the spiritual children of God. In addition, Christians confess that they are servants of God, therefore Colossians 3:22, "Servants, obey in all things your masters according to the flesh; not with eyeservice, as men-pleasers; but in singleness of heart, fearing God," applies to them as well. Finally, Christians enjoy the promise of Acts 5:32, "And we are his witnesses of these things; and so is also the Holy Ghost, whom God hath given to them that obey him," for their obedience.

The results and findings of the Christian participants surveyed are very interesting and informative. Since adherence to all five of these sermons is necessary in order to enjoy the fullness of the kingdom of heaven, it is important that all Christians know and understand them. The interesting part is that many Christians had been exposed to some of this information in spite of not knowing much about these sermons, especially the Olivet Discourse.

According to survey responses, the sermon that the participants were most obedient to is the Parables of the Kingdom. Nine percent of the survey participants reported that 90% of the time they obeyed the instructions given in this sermon, and only 10% of the time did they not obey. However, they reported this sermon third on the list of personally knowing what was in the sermon. This is an indication that they know more about this particular sermon than they think they know. This is a very good response; in fact, it is better than average. No other sermon enjoyed this level of obedience.

In the next group, 29% of the participants reported that 80% of the time they obeyed the Parables of the Kingdom. Twenty-four percent said that they obeyed Instructions to the Community at least 80% of the time. This is a very good response; however, it also means that 20% of the time they did not obey. It is notable that the Parables of the Kingdom, once again, scored highest in the first two highest levels of obedience and tied with another sermon in the third highest level. Seven percent of the participants obeyed the Olivet Discourse 80% of the time, and 2% obeyed the Instructions to the Twelve 80% of the time. No one obeyed the Sermon on the Mount at this level.

The next level of obedience is by far the largest group. Forty-three percent of the participants reported that they obeyed the Parables of the Kingdom and the Instructions to the Community 70% of the time. Forty-one percent obeyed the Olivet Discourse 70% of the time, 26% obeyed the Sermon on the Mount at least 70% of the time, and 17% obeyed the Instructions to the Twelve 70% of the time. This seems to be the norm for obedience of the Christian Torah, but it also indicates that they did not obey 30% of the time.

The next level indicates that this is the highest level of obedience of the Sermon on the Mount. Forty-eight percent of the participants reported that they obeyed the Sermon on the Mount at least 60% of the time. This group is almost 50% larger for the Sermon on the Mount than any other sermon. Twenty-nine percent obeyed the Olivet Discourse 60% of the time, 26% obeyed the Instructions to the Twelve, 21% obeyed the Instructions to the Community, and 9% obeyed the Parables of the Kingdom at this level. Of course all of these groups did not obey 40% of the time.

Thirty-six percent of the participants obeyed the Instructions to the Twelve at least 50% of the time, 24% obeyed the Sermon on the Mount 50% of the time, 17% obeyed the Olivet Discourse, 9% obeyed the Parables of the Kingdom, and 7% obeyed the Instructions to the Community at this level of obedience. The disobedience level for this group is 50%.

The final group of participants obeyed the Instructions to the Twelve at least 40% of the time. This means that 60% of the time they do not obey. Seventeen percent of the participants obeyed the Instructions to the Twelve at least 40% of the time, 4% obeyed the Olivet Discourse, and 2% obeyed the Instructions to the Community at the same level of obedience.

According to the survey results, most of the participants seem to be willing to obey Jesus according to their understanding of what they should be. This type of obedience is not easy, nor does it come quickly. It takes time to work out your soul's salvation. It requires training, teaching, preaching, and a commitment to personal study.

Many of the participants reported that they had heard something about each sermon to some degree—some to a large degree, some to a medium degree, and some very little.

The reasons for not knowing about the sermons or practicing what Jesus taught as recorded in each sermon were given as follows:

- Lack of teaching
- Lack of preaching
- Lack of personal study
- Inability to obey because of outside influences

The following charts show the results of the information flow of each sermon. Each chart shows the results of the knowledge base from all participants regarding each sermon. The first column indicates familiarity with the sermon. The next three columns indicate the reasons for receiving or not receiving information. These methods are teaching, preaching, or personal study. The colors on the columns indicate yes (green) and no (blue). The number inside of each column indicates the percentage who responded.

The first chart deals with the Sermon on the Mount. Notice that 83% reported that they were familiar with the sermon. Forty-six percent reported the reason of familiarity to be teaching, 49% reported preaching, and 46% reported personal study.

Only 19% had no information concerning this sermon. Five percent attributed lack of teaching to be the reason for not having more information, 7% reported preaching as the reason, and 17% reported personal study. The sample of other reasons is too insignificant for statistical reporting. This sermon is by far the most familiar.

Sermon Knowledge Results
Sermon on the Mount

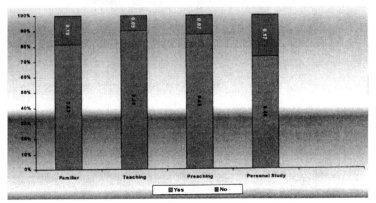

87

The next chart deals with the Instructions to the Twelve. This is the second most familiar sermon. For this sermon, 76% of the participants reported familiarity with this sermon. Forty-nine percent attributed that to teaching, 51% said preaching, and 49% personal study. Twenty-nine percent said that they are not familiar with this sermon. Seven percent gave teaching as the reason of unfamiliarity; 1% said preaching, and 27% said personal study.

Sermon Knowledge Results
Instructions to the Twelve

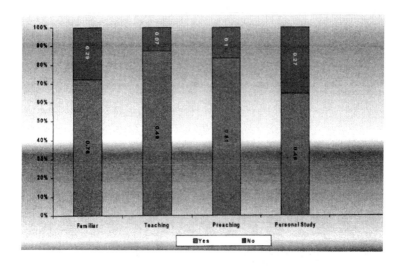

The Parables of the Kingdom sermon is discussed in the next chart. Seventy-one percent claimed familiarity with this sermon. Forty-six percent attributed their knowledge to teaching, 51% preaching, and 46% percent personal study. Twenty-nine percent claimed no familiarity with this sermon. Five percent attributed that to teaching, 7% to preaching, and 19% to personal study.

Sermon Knowledge Results
Parables of the Kingdom

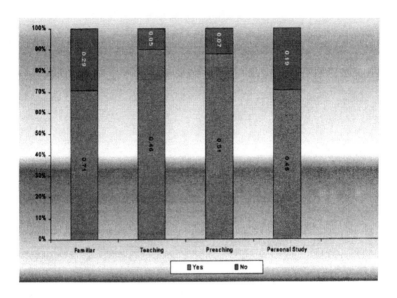

The next chart reports the findings regarding the Instructions to the Community sermon. Fewer than half of the participants have personal knowledge of this sermon. Only 44% of the participants reported familiarity with this sermon. Twenty-seven percent gave teaching as the reason for knowledge of the sermon, 34% gave preaching as the reason, and 27% said personal study. Fifty-eight percent admitted no familiarity of this sermon. Of those, 1% attributed no knowledge to teaching, 17% said preaching, and 46% said personal study.

Sermon Knowledge Results
Instructions to the Community

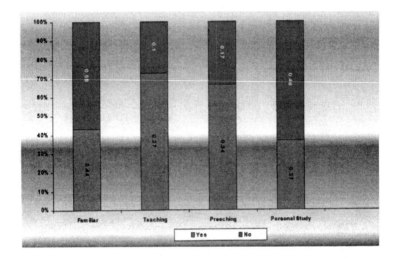

The final chart deals with the Olivet Discourse. This is the least-known sermon. Only 36% reported knowledge of this sermon. Twenty-four percent attributed their familiarity to teaching, 29% to preaching, and 24% to personal study. Sixty-six percent of the participants were not familiar with this sermon. One percent reported teaching as a reason for unfamiliarity, 17% said preaching, and 51% cited personal study.

Sermon Knowledge Results
Olivet Discourse

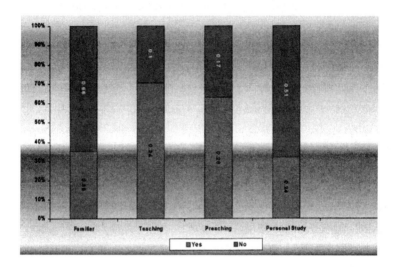

From this selected study of the Christian community we find that a large percentage of Christians do not know as much as they need to know about the Christian Torah. The survey results show that many of the survey participants in this statistical sample are familiar with the Sermon on the Mount, yet most are not able to apply the information that they have to their daily lives. Therefore, having the knowledge of the information does not seem to be sufficient for application.

The questions in the survey regarding this sermon are focused upon making Jesus' choices our first choice. One of the questions asked was, "How often do you select the Word of God as a basis for the choices that you make?" This is a very basic Christian principle, yet many survey participants are not able to live victorious lives in these areas because of lack of understanding. If you do not use the Word of God, the Devil does not listen to you. He only responds to the Word of God. In addition, if you make choices without considering what the Word of God has to say about that type of situation, you have a greater chance of getting into trouble.

Jesus does not want His followers to get tied up and trapped by sin. He left us clear instructions to begin to pattern our lives after His life. Christians believe that sometimes that there are no consequences for disobedience. Some believe that all they are doing when they disobey is giving up the blessing, and some blame God when they get in trouble. But someone said, and I agree, that sin will cause you to do more than you want to do, take you further than you want to go, and cause you to stay longer than you wanted to stay. Victory is ours every day if we obey Jesus and follow His teaching.

The survey also reported that many Christians have not had the teaching, preaching, or personal study that they desire concerning these five sermons. The surprising part was that most blame themselves for not studying the Bible in that area.

The majority of the survey participants disobeyed Jesus' teaching almost 50% of the time. This is not to say that people do not make mistakes, because no one obeys absolutely everything that he or she should. However, the older you get in Christ, the more mature you should be, and the less the Devil should be able to do the same old things he used to do. The Devil does not know anything new; therefore, sooner of later it should be more difficult for Christians to be defeated in certain areas. For instance, the Parables of the Kingdom have to do more with the character of the Kingdom than the character of a person. Survey participants seem to know more about how the kingdom operates that they do about how they should operate.

Kingdom parables ranked highest in the three highest categories of obedience. Yet the Sermon on the Mount, the sermon that addresses the character and attitude of the individual, does not even show up in the top two highest levels of obedience. It will be difficult for a Christian to get though the persecutions that come with following Christ and for His sake if the Christians do not know that persecution is a part of Christian life.

Many Christians think that people should not lie to them, and they get offended and often stay too long in a state of unforgiveness. The Bible is very clear about what happened to Jesus at the hands of those who did not follow or believe Him. Jesus said that the servant is not greater than the master, so if they persecuted me, they will persecute you also. This information is made very clear in the Sermon on the Mount. This is not the only place to find such information, but knowing what Jesus said certainly helps put offense and rejection into proper perspective.

The Instructions to the Twelve showed up in the second highest obedience level, but it was such a small percentage that ranked in this category. The majority of the sample group ended up at a lower level of obedience. Jesus gives specific instructions regarding how to operate on assignment from Him. Jesus specifically stated in this sermon (Matt. 10:18–22) that they will be brought before governors and kings for His sake, for a testimony against them and the Gentiles. Then He told them that those same people would deliver them up, but to take no thought how or what they speak because the words to say would be given to them in that same hour. He told them that they are not the one who will be speaking. He said that the Spirit of our Father speaks in them.

Now He told them that brother shall deliver up brother to death, and the father the child; the children shall rise up against their parents and cause them to be put to death. This is the statement that many Christians miss. He told them, "You shall be hated of all men for His name's sake; but you that endure to the end shall be saved." These are clear instructions about what will happen when Christians go out to witness or out on the mission field. It is important for Christians to know this because many of them believe that God speaks out of the pastor's mouth, or the minister's or any other church leader's, but not the mouth of the average Christian.

Jesus told them that some of their own family would not support them if they followed Him. In addition, He said, they would be hated. He wanted them to understand that the world loves the world, and it hates God and His kingdom. Therefore, those who are a part of Him will be hated. It is very important to understand what Jesus is saying in this sermon.

Many of the Christian authors and theologians included in this study agree that these five sermons are very important. They have provided a multitude of material saying the same thing: **Study these sermons and grow up in the things of God.**

CHAPTER 5

IMPROVING KINGDOM LIVING TODAY

Generally, the participants of the survey are familiar with all five of the sermons, but they do not have an intimate knowledge of all of them. The Sermon on the Mount is the one that they have the most knowledge of, but their lives do not reflect that knowledge. Based upon questionnaire answers, the reason for this is that they do not clearly understand how the sermon relates to current-day situations and relationships.

The Parables of the Kingdom and the Instructions to the Community are the two sermons that the study group most closely followed. They did not know as much about these sermons as they knew about the Sermon on the Mount, but what they knew they used in their daily lives.

The Instructions to the Twelve and the Olivet Discourse were the least understood, and, after the Sermon on the Mount, the least followed. Based on the survey data, the major reason for that is the lack of teaching, preaching, or personal study of these sermons. Some did give personal reasons such as never hearing the name Olivet Discourse or being married to an unsaved spouse.

The apostle Paul, and some of the other apostles who are New Testament authors, wrote Epistles that included explanations of some of what Jesus said in these five sermons. This caused some people to know more about these sermons even though they had not studied them personally. However, there is nothing like knowing what Jesus said for you to do. Their writings should improve and increase your knowledge as they provide a detailed explanation or a statement of doctrine concerning what Jesus commanded.

Overall, the knowledge of the sermons by the community of believers that participated in this study is very impressive. The level of obedience is greater than even the survey participants expected. Yet, Jesus wants us to live a full and victorious life. He knew that once we became born again, we were a part of the family of God instantly. But growing up in God would take some time, in fact a lifetime, because God is progressive and He will keep us growing as long as we are willing and teachable.

I recommend the following activities to improve the knowledge, practice, and obedience to the teaching of Jesus in these five sermons:

1. Children should be taught these sermons at an early age in Sunday school classes or in a setting such as Vacation Bible School and children's church.
2. These sermons should be taught to adults and children frequently in weekly Bible studies, or at least once a year in other training opportunities, until the subject matter is learned and practiced.
3. Special workshops should be designed to facilitate learning and using the principles found in each of these sermons.
4. The principles found in these sermons should be incorporated into weekly sermons at least once a quarter.
5. The principles of each sermon should be included in printed teaching materials such as Sunday school books.

6. Explain and teach these kingdom principles to new converts as a part of the teaching in new members classes.
7. Church leaders should practice these principles by example because many in the congregations need role models to follow.

Thank you, Holy Spirit, for helping me
to write and prepare this book!

I have included a questionnaire that is designed to test your knowledge of the Christian Torah.

QUESTIONNAIRE

FOR CHRISTIANS ONLY!

This questionnaire is designed to test your knowledge of the Christian Torah. There are questions relating to each of the five sermons of the Christian Torah. At the end of the questionnaire, you can score your results according to a grading scale.

Please answer the following questions with a number from 1 to 5 according to the following criteria:

1 = never
2 = seldom
3 = sometimes
4 = most of the time
5 = all of the time

The Sermon on the Mount

1. _____ How often would you be willing to give away something that you need for sustaining your life such as cars, clothes, houses, or furniture, depending solely on Jesus Christ for your subsistence?

2. _____ How often do you depend solely upon God for all of your material needs and resources (material, physical, temporal, emotional, relational, psychological, emotional, etc.)?

3. _____ How often do you depend on God solely for your fundamental needs and resources (water, energy, food, clothing, livelihood, medical and dental care, transporta tion, leisure activities, safe environment, shelter mobility, etc.)?

4. _____ How often are you saddened, sorrowful, or on the verge of tears when you encounter, recognize, or partic- ipate in sin?

5. _____ How often do you examine yourself to locate sin present in your life and turn from that as a result of your findings, no matter how small the sin?

6. _____ How often should a person expect to be the loser in any given situation?

7. _____ How often do you select the Word of God as a basis for the choices that you make?

8. _____ When you believe that you have heard God's direction on an issue, how often do you obey?

9. _____ How often do you hunger to study God's Word so passionately that you can hardly wait until the next opportunity?

10. _____ How often do you extend mercy to people who do not want or deserve it?

11. _____ How often do you apologize to people who are in the wrong when you know that they are wrong?

12. _____ How often are you honest about whether or not you like something, rather than pretending that you feel differently just to please family or friends?

13. _____ How often do you tell people the truth, even if telling them means they will be able to take advantage of you?

14. _____ How often do you find yourself suffering for what is right according to the Word of God?

15. _____ How often do you accept criticism without reacting defensively or feeling self-pity?

16. _____ How often do you believe that it is wrong to compromise your principles to keep people from taking advantage of you?

17. _____ How often are you the one who tries to make amends in relationships that are being strained between a friend, family member, co-worker or Christian sister or brother?

18. _____ How often do you refuse to allow your anger to cause you to call your sister or brother in Christ an unfriendly name (by word or thought)?

19. _____ Do you believe that people who say bad things about Christian brothers or sisters, in a state of anger, actually murder them?

20. _____ How often do you rejoice when people tell lies about you, persecute you, and say all kinds of evil things

against you because you refuse to compromise your character or integrity as taught in the Word of God?

21. _____ If all the people whom you have met in the last year say to you that they want to follow you because they want to be more like Christ, how often would you be pleased to know that they will get the correct image by watching you?

22. _____ Do you think that married people who look at (silently admire or become attracted to) people other than their spouses commit adultery?

23. _____ Should Christians who believe that they missed God and married the wrong person stay married (not get a divorce)?

24. _____ How often should a person refuse to swear to prove a point when he knows that he is correct in what he believes?

25. _____ Do you think that it is a bad idea to say whatever is necessary to shut people up, especially noisy, talkative people?

26. _____ How often do you worry about things (circumstances) that happen in your life?

27. _____ If a person in authority over you (such as your boss) asks you to tell a lie or be in agreement with a lie being told, how often will you say, "No"?

28. _____ How often should a person get forgiveness for something that he or she has done, instead of getting payback?

29. _____ Once you give your word to someone, how often do you keep your word, even when unexpected circumstances come up that cause you to change what you said?

30. _____ How often do you prefer that God would bless your enemies over blessing you?

31. _____ How often do you pray for your enemies?

32. _____ If a person tries to force you to do something to help him or her, how often do you refuse to allow that to happen to you or your family?

33. _____ How often do you secretly give gifts, food, clothes, and money, etc., to people in need?

34. _____ Do you include special time with God in prayer as a part of your daily activities?

35. _____ Is fasting something that you do on a regular basis?

36. _____ Do your bank accounts show more activity in giving to God and the kingdom of God than your earthly need?

37. _____ How often do you believe that people who do wrong repeatedly (as a result of their own fault) should be forgiven of the fault?

38. _____ How often do you give people gifts, not expecting anything in return—not even a thank you?

39. _____ How often do you continue to try to convince people (of your commitment to Christ) who are not interested in your conversation and who don't want anyone else to listen to you?

40. _____ How often do you treat people the same way in which you want to be treated?

41. _____ How often do you believe that everything that you do will come back to you in the same way in which you did it?

42. _____ How often do you make Jesus Christ the foundation of everything that you do or say?

Instructions to the Twelve

43. _____ How often do you go out to seek the lost?

44. _____ How often do you get offended because people will not listen to the Gospel?

45. _____ Do you ever feel rejected when people reject you when you are witnessing to them about the good news?

46. _____ How often do you tell people about the kingdom of heaven or the kingdom of God?

47. _____ When you speak, preach, teach, or witness to people concerning the Gospel or the things of God, how often do you expect the Holy Spirit to do all of the talking?

48. _____ How often do you expect men to hate you because of your love for Christ?

49. _____ How often do you position yourself to be a servant to other people?

50. _____ How often do you think that you should be the servant, versus the one served?

51. _____ How often do you believe that people should be forgiven for their decisions and behavior, instead of being judged for every action?

Parables of the Kingdom

52. _____ When you hear new revelation from the Word of God, how often do you make that Word a part of your life?

53. _____ How often do you understand what is being preached and taught during Sunday services or Bible study?

54. _____ How often does the revelation or understanding of the Word of God free you from problems, cares, or habitual things that you desire to stop?

55. _____ How often do you repent and correct things in your life that you know do not please the Lord, versus putting it off?

56. _____ How often do you believe that God shares His secrets with you?

57. _____ How often do you stand on the Word of God, no matter what people are saying?

58. _____ How often do you stand on the Word of God during crisis, times of trouble, or unusual negative circumstances?

59. _____ How often do you practice God's principles (such as giving your tithe) above all that you need or want in this life?

Instructions to the Community

60. _____ How often do you trust God when you are going through something and it seems that God is nowhere around?

61. _____ How often do you seek to help save the lost without counting the cost to yourself (such as going into a heavy crime area to find the lost)?

62. _____ Do you forgive people unconditionally no matter how many times they hurt you?

63. _____ How often should people forgive people who continually commit terrible acts of crimes or sins against them?

64. _____ How often do you let your Christian brothers or sisters know when they have sinned against you?

65. _____ How often would you exercise your right to go to the church with two or more witnesses if the brother or sister does not listen to you?

66. _____ How often would you prefer mercy and compassion for those who do not deserve either?

67. _____ How often would you gather with a brother or sister to invoke the presence of God for a common concern?

68. _____ How often do you use the power of agreement to accomplish a purpose or goal?

69. _____ Before you judge people, how often do you consider that people's intentions were probably much better than the deeds they committed?

The Olivet Discourse

70. _____ How often are you willing to help another person do what God has given them to do and put your vision or mission on hold?

71. _____ How often do you conduct your daily business as if Christ is coming back any day now?

72. _____ How often are you more faithful over another person's business than your own?

73. _____ How often do you procrastinate about doing what it takes in order for you to advance in the things of God (to grow up)?

74. _____ How often do you serve doing the work of the kingdom of God as if this will be your last opportunity?

75. _____ How often do you take every opportunity to be the best steward of what God has entrusted to you have and to do?

76. _____ Since you have been saved, how often have you multiplied the talents (money, spiritual gifts, etc.) that God has given you?

77. _____ How often do you feed the hungry?

78. _____ How often do you help the poor and homeless?

79. _____ How often do you support prison ministry in any way (money, time, or talent)?

80. _____ How often do you speak a kind word to a stranger?

81. _____ How often do you consider your brothers and sisters in Christ as your close family members?

82. _____ How often do you consider yourself being led by the Holy Spirit?

83. _____ How often do you make kindness your first choice?

84. _____ How often do you believe that you operate in kingdom principles?

85. _____ How often do you believe that you receive comfort when you need comforting?

86. _____ How often do you receive new revelations from the Word of God?

87. _____How often do you give to people who have nothing to give back to you?

88. _____Are you familiar with the following sermons found in Matthew? Give yourself 5 points for each "yes" answer and 1 point for each "no."

The Sermon on the Mount (Matt. 5:1–7:27): _____yes/no

Instructions to the Twelve (Matt. 9:35–10:42): _____ yes/no

Parables of the Kingdom (Matt. 13:1–52): _____ yes/no

Instructions to the Community (Matt. 18:1–35): _____ yes/no

The Olivet Discourse (Matt. 24:1–25:46): _____ yes/no

Grading Scale
(0–460 points possible)

460 points	Excellent
368—459 points	Outstanding
184—367 points	Good
93—183 points	Average
0—92 points	Poor

NOTES

1.   Edwin K. Broadhead, *Demand and Grace: The Sermon On The Mount* (Macon, Georgia: Smyth & Helwys Publishing, Inc, 1999), 17.

2.   Bill Dodds and Michael J. Dodds, *Happily Ever After Begins Here and Now: Living the Beatitudes Today* (Chicago: Loyola Press 1997).

3.   Bill Dodds and Michael J. Dodds, *Happily Ever After Begins Here and Now: Living the Beatitudes Today* (Chicago: Loyola Press 1997).

4.   Stuart Briscoe, *The Sermon on the Mount: Daring to Be Different* (Colorado Springs, CO: Shaw Books, 1995).

5.   Sinclair Ferguson, *Sermon on the Mount: Kingdom Life in a Fallen World* (Carlisle, PA: Banner Of Truth, 1987), 21.

6.   Michael H. Crosby, *Spirituality of the Beatitudes: Matthew's Challenge For First World Christians*, (Mary Knoll, NY: Orbis Books, 2000), 140.

7.   Richard Peace, Layman Coleman, Andrew Sloan, Cathy Tardit. *Sermon On The Mount: Examining Your Life* (Littletown, CO: Serendipity House, 1984), 26.

8.   Richard Peace, Layman Coleman, Andrew Sloan, Cathy Tardit. *Sermon On The Mount: Examining Your Life* (Littletown, CO: Serendipity House, 1984), 26.

9.   Michael H. Crosby, *Spirituality of the Beatitudes: Matthew's Challenge For First World Christians*, (Mary Knoll, NY: Orbis Books, 2000).

10. Robert Farrar Capon, *The Parables of the Kingdom* (Grand Rapids: Eerdmans Publishing Co., 1991).

11. Robert Farrar Capon, *The Parables of the Kingdom* (Grand Rapids: Eerdmans Publishing Co., 1991), 157.

12. Duncan Carr, *Thirty-One Days In The Kingdom of God*, (Hagerstown, MD: Fairmont Books, 2000), 16.

13. Alfred J. Church, *The Story of the Last Days of Jerusalem: From Josephus* (London: 1880).

14. Alfred J. Church, *The Story of the Last Days of Jerusalem: From Josephus* (London: 1880).

15. Thomas Nelson, *The Word In Life Study Bible*, (Nashville: Thomas Nelson Publishers, 1993), 2079.

16. Bill Dodds and Michael J. Dodds, *Happily Ever After Begins Here and Now: Living The Beatitudes Today*, (Chicago: Loyola Press 1997).

17. Arthur W. Pink, *An Exposition of the Sermon on the Mount* (Swengel, Pennsylvania: I. G. Herendeen, 1953).

18. Sinclair Ferguson, *Sermon on the Mount: Kingdom Life in a Fallen World* (Carlisle, PA: Banner Of Truth, 1987).

19. Warren Wiersbe, *Live Like a King: How to Develop a Royal Lifestyle From the Beatitudes* (Grand Rapids, Mich.: Kregel Publications, 1976).

20. Pat Robertson, *The Secret Kingdom* (Dallas: World Publishing, 1992).

21. Edwin K. Broadhead, *Demand and Grace: The Sermon on the Mount* (Macon, Georgia: Smyth & Helwys Publishing, Inc, 1999).

GLOSSARY

Abundant Living—Living in heart, mind, and soul exceedingly above natural aspects of the earth, both spiritually and naturally.

Analysis—An examination of things to determine their elements or parts and a statement showing the result of the examination.

Antitheses—The opposition or contrast of ideas; the direct opposite.

Christians—Followers of Christ. Jesus' disciples were first called Christians in Antioch (Acts 11:26); King Agrippa called followers of Christ Christians in Acts 26:28, and in 1 Peter 4:16, Peter called Christians followers of Christ. Christians are people who believe that Jesus was crucified, died, was buried, and rose from the dead by the power of the Father, and they have confessed their belief with their mouth.

Christian Torah—The moral and spiritual instructions that are written in the five sermons that Jesus Christ preached in the gospel of Matthew (also found in Luke 6:20–49, Luke 9:1–6, Mark 4:1–20, Luke 8:4–15, Mark 9:33–37, Luke 9:46–48, Mark 13:1–13, and Luke 21.) These instructions give direction to Christians concerning living in the kingdom of heaven and how to be in relationship with God, with one another, with the unsaved, and with the community locally and universally.

Compliance—Willingness to please and be in agreement with an act or action taken.

Current-day Christians—People who are living today who call themselves followers of Christ. Current-day Christians refer to themselves as Christians just as the early Christians of the early church. The additional names "believers" (Acts 5:14), "brothers" (Acts 6:3), and "saints" (Acts 9:13) also continue to be used.

Daily lives—A habitual way of life that is practiced daily as a part of living from the morning of one day to the morning of the next day for a lifetime. This practice is something that is embedded in the lifestyle of the individuals.

Death—A term that denotes the extinction of vital functions, so that their renewal is impossible, or the end of life, as in a state of being dead. Death is defined by separation. Since God is the giver of life, there is no life without Him. Therefore, being separated from God is death.

Discourse—A Latin term that means conversation or a presentation of a particular point of view of the presenter. It is also an augment for or against an issue of concern.

Eternal existence—Endless existence that all possess, saved as well as unsaved.

Eternal life—The state of living for all eternity with God. A person begins this living process as soon as he or she accepts Jesus Christ as personal Savior and Lord. This is a wonderful gift from God.

Evaluation—An appraised value of a situation, thing, or person.

Everlasting—This means enduring forever and lasting forever (an eternal time). The Greek meaning of everlasting is "age-lasting."

Gospel—The good news of salvation in Christ. The word "gospel" is a Greek word that means "a reward for bringing good news" or "good news." Jesus pronounced in His sermon in Nazareth that He was anointed to preach the gospel to the poor (Luke 4:18).

Gospel of Matthew—This is the first book in the New Testament. It is the good news presenting Jesus as the Messiah and King. It is written by Matthew, a follower and a disciple of Jesus who was a tax collector and who became one of the twelve apostles of Jesus (Matt. 9:9). The gospel of Matthew is divided into five main sections, each consisting of the preaching and teaching of Jesus. It also consists of stories of Jesus' life and the works associated with His preaching and teaching.

Hebrew people (Hebrews)—A term that is used to describe the ancestry of the Jewish people, also known as the nation of Israel. Abram, later known as Abraham, was called this first in Genesis 14:13. After this, Abraham's descendants who came through Isaac and Jacob were known as Hebrews (Gen. 40:15; 43:32).

Hebrew Torah—The first five canonical books of the Old Testament, written by Moses, that embrace the whole body of religious literature of Judaism inherited from the prophets, priests, and elders. It is composed of specific applications of how to relate to God, how to live a godly life, and how to be in relationship with each other and the community at large.

Instructions—A command or order to follow knowledge or information given or taught, or giving directions, commands, or precepts to follow as taught.

Kingdom—A place where a king rules. The king is sovereign and has rule and authority over people and places. *Vines Dictionary* gives this definition as used in the New Testament. According to *Vines*, kingdom is the Greek word "basileia" and is primarily an abstract noun denoting "sovereignty, royal power" and is translated literally as the territory or people over whom a king rules, as, for example, in Matthew 4:8 and Mark 3:24. It is used especially of the "kingdom" of God and of Christ.

Kingdom of God—Embraces all created intelligences, both in heaven and in earth. All of the residents willingly subject and submit themselves to God and thus are in fellowship with God. The kingdom is mentioned mostly in the gospels of Matthew, Mark, and Luke. The gospel of John and the epistles of the New Testament refer to the kingdom as it relates to eternal life or salvation. The apostle Paul describes the kingdom of God as "righteousness, and peace, and joy in the Holy Ghost" (Rom. 14:17). The kingdom of God is the place where Christ reigns; no evil can prevail in this kingdom. The gospels of Matthew, Mark, and Luke focus on the present aspect of the kingdom of God, but these gospels make it clear that the kingdom of God will be realized perfectly in the second coming of Christ.

Kingdom of heaven—A spiritual place that Jesus Christ has prepared for all who believe in Him and in His name. It contains a high standard of ethics and righteousness afforded by death and resurrection of Christ. It comes through the ministry of Jesus Christ and is considered a mystery even though it is fully explained in the gospels. It is the place where Christians reside in this world but not of this world. The kingdom of heaven is used interchangeably with the kingdom of God. In parallel passages Matthew uses the "kingdom of heaven," whereas Luke and Mark use the "kingdom of God" (Matt. 4:17, Luke 13:28, Mark 1:15). Matthew also uses these terms interchangeably at times, as seen in Matthew 19:23–24.

Kings—Rulers of nations or a state usually called a kingdom.

Life—The physical functions (capacity for metabolism, growth and reaction to stimuli, and reproduction) of people, animals, and plants. In physical terms, life is the time between birth and death. Because God is the source of life, it is a gift from Him.

Lords—Persons having great power and authority; rulers or masters who are the head of state.

Millennium kingdom—Theological term based upon Revelation 20, indicating the thousand-year period of Christ's future reign on the earth in connection with the establishment of the kingdom over Israel (Acts 1:6). Basically, however, it is more accurate to employ the term "kingdom," which has far-reaching roots in the Old Testament, rather than a term signifying merely a time during which the kingdom continues. For the purpose of this research, the millennium kingdom occurs according to the premillennialism theological view that the age will end in judgment at the second coming of Christ, who will restore the kingdom to Israel and reign for at least one thousand years The millennium will be the last of the ordered ages of time. Eternity will not dawn until the millennium is complete (Isa. 65:17; Isa. 66:22; 2 Peter 3:13; Rev. 21:1).

Millennium Kingdom of God—The dispensations of the reign of Jesus Christ for one thousand years as the king of the nation of Israel. This is a time when the church dispensation of grace will be over, and the church will reign with Christ.

Natural life—Life that has a beginning and an ending. The natural life ending for one who is separated from God results in being separated eternally from God in the lake of fire, whereas the natural life ending of one who is with God results in being with God for all eternity. Thus, separation from God is eternal death; being with God is eternal life.

New Testament—This is the last will and testament (covenant) of Jesus Christ to His followers. It is the second part of two major parts of the Bible. It tells the good news of the gospel of Jesus Christ that includes His birth, life, ministry, death, and resurrection. It also includes the establishment and early growth of the church, as well as the revelation of the eternal position and place of God's people.

Old Testament—This is the covenant that God made between Himself and His people, the nation of Israel. It begins with God and His creation of all that is in existence in the universe. It describes the acts and the ways of God through the relationship of God and His people. At the end of this covenant there was a short break of approximately four hundred years before the establishment of the new covenant of the New Testament.

Public ministry—The time and duration of the ministry of Jesus Christ to the public that began with His beginning to operate as priest and King and culminated in His death and resurrection as Savior and Lord.

Repentance—Turning away from sin, disobedience, or rebellion and turning back to God; changing from what is currently being done because of remorse or regret for past conduct that causes one to be sorry for sin, and turning around and going in the opposite direction.

Sanhedrin—A seventy-member council that operated as the highest ruling body and court of justice among the Jewish people in the time of Jesus. Headed by the high priest of Israel, the Sanhedrin enjoyed some degree of power over certain religious, civil, and criminal matters by the foreign nations that dominated the land of Israel at various times in its history.

Super-thesis—The intensifying of an idea; a greater measure of an idea.

The Olivet Discourse—This sermon discusses the end time events and the triumphant return of Christ.

The Sermon Giving Instructions to the Community—Jesus gives instructions on the spiritual and social conduct of Christians with regard to other people and the community at large.

The Sermon on the Instructions to the Twelve—Jesus selected twelve disciples, appointed them as apostles, and prepared them to do the work of His ministry. The work of His ministry included having the authority to drive out evil spirits and to heal every disease. This is the sermon Jesus used to instruct them about how to conduct themselves when they were sent out to minister.

The Sermon on the Mount—This is an explanation of what Jesus wanted His followers to be and to do. In other words, how should Christians conduct themselves in their relationship to God, to fellow believers, and to other people? This sermon contains information that sets the standard of Christian character and influence. The moral laws of God are clearly stated in this sermon.

These moral laws include, but are not limited to, the Christians' prayer, the ambitions of Christians, and the relationships that Christians have with their brothers, with their Father, and with others. Christian conduct is paramount in God's Kingdom.

The Sermon of Parables of the Kingdom—In this sermon, Jesus teaches the operation and character of the kingdom. It contains natural and spiritual principles. If these principle truths are obeyed, then the quality of life for Christians is abundantly blessed. This is what God intended for His people. Being passive does not change the negative consequences for not obeying. If the principles are not obeyed, then the results are quite different from what is expected.

BIBLIOGRAPHY

Bickel, Bruce and Jantz. *Guide To The End of the World.* Eugene, Oregon: Harvest House Publishers, 1999.

Bright, John. *The Kingdom of God (Hebrew History from its Early Old Testament Times).* Nashville: Abingdom Press, 1981.

Briscoe, Stuart. *The Sermon on the Mount: Daring to Be Different.* Colorado Springs, Colo.: Shaw Books, 1995.

Broadhead, Edwin K. *Demand and Grace: The Sermon on the Mount.* Macon, Georgia: Smyth & Helwys Publishing, Inc., 1999.

Capon, Robert Farrar. *The Parables of the Kingdom.* Grand Rapids: Eerdmans Publishing Co., 1991.

Carson, D. A. *Jesus' Sermon on the Mount And His Confrontation with the World.* Grand Rapids: Global Christian Publishers, 1999.

Carr, Duncan. *Thirty-One Days In The Kingdom of God.* Hagerstown, Md.: Fairmont Books, 2000.

Chambers, Oswald. *Studies in the Sermon on the Mount.* Grand Rapids: Barbour Publishing, 1960.

Church, Alfred J. *The Story of the Last Days of Jerusalem, from Josephus.* London: 1880.

Conn, Harvie. *Urban Ministry: The Kingdom of God, the City & the People of God.* Downers Grove, Ill.: Inter-Varsity Press, 1984.

Crosby, Michael H. *Spirituality of the Beatitudes: Matthew's Challenge For First World Christians.* Mary Knoll, New York: Orbis Books, 2000.

Danby, H. trans. *The Mishnah.* (1933), pp. 446–61; E. K. J. Rosenthal, ed., *Law and Religion* (1938), 3:50–53, 62.

Dodds, Bill and Dodds, Michael J. *Happily Ever After Begins Here and Now: Living the Beatitudes Today.* Chicago: Loyola Press, 1997.

Ferguson, Sinclair. *Sermon on the Mount: Kingdom Life in a Fallen World.* Carlisle, Penn.: Banner Of Truth, 1987.

Fuellenbach, John. *The Kingdom of God: The Message of Jesus Today.* Maryknoll, New York: Orgis Gooks, 1995.

Hayford. *God's Way to Wholeness—Divine Healing by the Power of the Holy Spirit, Spirit-Filled Life Kingdom Dynamics Study Guide.* Nashville: Thomas Nelson, 1993.

Jeffrey, Grant R. *Triumphant Return: The Coming Kingdom of God.* Canada: Frontier Research Publications Inc., 2001.

Ladd, Eldon George. *The Gospel of the Kingdom: Scriptural Studies in the Kingdom of God.* Grand Rapids, Michigan: Erdmans Publishing Co., 1959.

LeMasters, Phillip. *Discipleship for All Believers: Christian Ethics & the Kingdom of God.* Scottdale, Pennsylvania: Herald Press, 1964.

Lloyd-Jones, Martyn. *The Kingdom of God.* Wheaton, Ill.: Good News Publishers, 1992.

McVey, Steve. *Living in the Kingdom of God Where Grace Rules,* Eugene, Oregon: Harvest House Publishers, 1998.

Moltmann, Jurgen. *The Trinity and the Kingdom of God.* Augsburg: Fortress, 1981.

Nelson's Illustrated Bible Dictionary. Thomas Nelson, 1988.

The New Unger's Bible Dictionary. Moody Press Chicago, Illinois: 1988.

Patte, Daniel. *Discipleship According to the Sermon on the Mount.* Valley Forge: Trinity Press International, 1996.

Peace, Richard. Coleman, Lyman, Sloan, Andrew, Tardit, Cathy. *Sermon On The Mount: Examining Your Life.* Littletown, Colo.: Serendipity House, 1984.

Pink, Arthur W. *An Exposition of the Sermon on the Mount.* Swengel, Penn.: I.G. Herendeen, 1953.

Ridderbos, Herman. *The Coming of the Kingdom.* Philadelphia, Penn.: The Presbyterian and Reformed Publishing company, 1962.

Robertson, Pat. *The Secret Kingdom.* Dallas: World Publishing, 1992.

Schaap, Ward. *The Character of the Kingdom: Studies in the Parables.* Grand Rapids: Baker-Revell, 1984.

Stott, John R.W., *The Message of the Sermon on the Mount, The Bible Speaks Today.* Downers Grove, Illinois: Inter-Varsity Press, 1978.

The Word In Life Study Bible. Nashville, Tenn.: Thomas Nelson Publishers, 1996.

Wiebe, Ben, *Messianic Ethics: Jesus' Proclamation of the Kingdom of God & the Church in Response.* Scottdale, Penn.: Herald Press, 1992.

Wiersbe, Warren. *Live Like a King: How to Develop a Royal Lifestyle From the Beatitudes.* Grand Rapids, Mich.: Kregel Publications, 1976.

Worth, Roland H. Jr. *The Sermon on the Mount: Its Old Testament Roots.* Mahwah, New York: Paulist Press, 1997.

ABOUT THE AUTHOR

Dr. Cynthia V. White is a native of Macon, Georgia. She is the daughter of the late Rev. Lee A. and Sallie Townes. She is a widow, the mother of six children, and the grandmother of nine grandchildren.

Dr. White graduated from Ballard Hudson High School in Macon, Georgia and continued her education at Morris Brown College in Atlanta, Georgia, where she received a Bachelor of Science Degree in Mathematics and Education. In May 1999 she received the degree of Master of Arts in Biblical Studies of the Old Testament from Maple Springs Baptist Bible College and Seminary, Capitol Heights, Maryland. In May 2002, she received her doctorate degree from the same college.

After 31 years of dedicated service, Dr. White retired from the Department of the Navy in January of 1999. During her tenure there she served as the head of the Computer Aided Design and Manufacturing Department, the Industrial Improvement Technologies Department, the Joint Electronic Drawings and Manufacturing of Industrial Data Department, and the Military Construction Projects Department. She also served as the Program Manager for the Service Craft Management and Manufacturing Technology Department for the Naval Shipyards.

Dr. White is a strong supporter of community services. She has participated in fundraisers for the March of Dimes, she supports children in need programs, and she is a former member of the Board of Directors for the Center for Community Development of Housing for the Mentally Ill and the Aged. Adding to her extensive resume of charitable work, Dr. White is also a former member of the Board of Directors and served as the Secretary of Bethel House, a community support center for people in need of help such as food, housing, education, and jobs.

During her Christian journey, Dr. White has taught in several venues, including Sunday School, Vacation Bible School, Bible studies, workshops and conferences, and other Christian settings. She has also served as a member of the choir and steward board.

Currently, Dr. White serves an ordained Elder of God Is in Control Church in Waldorf, Maryland under the leadership of Bishop Elect Rodney and Elder Betty Walker. As a member and leader, she serves as Chief Elder in the Apostolic, Secretary of Church Finances, Church Administrator, a member of the Praise and Worship team, a member of Another Touch of Glory Covenant Ministries School of the Prophets Board of Presbyters, and a valued member of the God Is In Control Church Ministerial/Administrative Staff and the Another Touch of Glory Covenant Ministries Staff.

Dr. White is also the owner and CEO of a recently established business "Fruit That Remain, LLC," a company designed to provide new businesses with structure, vision, and direction and to assist established business owners with products and services that will contribute to their success and help them accomplish the particular goals and objectives they have set forth for their business.

Above all, Apostle White is a child of the living God who has been gifted to teach the word of God with power and demonstration, to declare the will of God with clarity and precise articulation, and to love the unloveable as Christ loves us!

CONTACT INFORMATION

To contact Dr. Cynthia V. White, please write to:

Dr. Cynthia V. White
1282 Smallwood Drive West #195
Waldorf, Maryland 20603
Phone: (301) 442-3116

For more information about Fruit That Remain, LLC, please contact us at:

Fruit That Remain, LLC
1282 Smallwood Drive West #195
Waldorf, Maryland 20603
Phone: (301) 868-4314
Fax: (301) 868-7326
www.fruitthatremain.com

Other Works by the Author:

Understanding Spiritual Maturity

In this book, you will be able to determine where you are in your Christian walk and what victories and pitfalls you should expect with each stage of development. Although this work is Christian in nature, you will also find several theoretical studies that support the various stages of spiritual maturity. Spiritually speaking, are you a baby, a young child, a young man, a young adult, or a spiritual father? As you read this book, you will find the answer to this question and many more.

What Your Father Never Told You...About Business

This booklet is designed to provoke you into thinking about some of the requirements not often discussed by others, but are essential in understanding the risks and the costs of operating a successful business. Each administrative key point is posed in a question format and will be beneficial before starting and going through the various life cycles of your business success. Also available in CD format.

To order additional books or CDs, contact Fruit That Remain Publishing using the contact information above.